Net Curiosity Score

Boost your Innovation
with this New KPI

Rik Vera

Lannoo Campus

D/2024/45/551 – ISBN 978 90 209 54456 – NUR 800

Cover and interior design: Atelier Steve Reynders

© Rik Vera & Lannoo Publishers nv, Tielt, 2024.

LannooCampus Publishers is a subsidiary of Lannoo Publishers, the book and multimedia division of Lannoo Publishers nv.

All rights reserved.
No part of this publication may be reproduced and/or made public, by means of printing, photocopying, microfilm or any other means, without the prior written permission of the publisher.

LannooCampus Publishers
Vaartkom 41 box 01.02
3000 Leuven
Belgium
www.lannoocampus.com

P.O. Box 23202
1100 DS Amsterdam
The Netherlands

Contents

Foreword 11
Cycling Route Network 17
    #0   Cycling Junctions.. 17
    #1   *Mulholland Drive* and *The OA* 17

Cycling Route Network 'The Importance of Curiosity' 21

Route 'Alice in Wonderland' 21
    #2   Boosting curiosity is boosting profitability 21
    #3   A Life in Lyrics... 23
    #4   Roll Up, Roll Up 24
    #5   Parallel World 26
    #6   Chernobyl Syndrome or Conscious Blindness 28
    #7   Bitterballen and Buttermilk, My New Content.............. 39

Curiosity or a Tsunami Ambush?.. 31
    #8   Beach Chair Syndrome..31
    #9   Towering Wave of Resistance to Change......................... 32
    #10   A True 4000 Holes: Measuring for the Sake of Measuring...33
    #11   Porter's Five as Kindling... 34
    #12   Cars on the Beach or Standing on the Surfboard.................. 35
    #13   Heading Out to the Open Ocean – Because You Must 37

Houston, we have a problem 38
    #14   Outside Your and My Comfort Zone................................ 38
    #15   Defeating the Big Bad Monster... 39
    #16   The Third Thing, a Valuable Discovery 40
    #17   Superpower, the Child Awakens....................................... 41
    #18   Gentle Bell Curves vs. Shark Fins: Tsunamis in
           Wonderland 43
    #19   Advanced Tightrope Walking: No Risk = The Biggest Risk ..45

Cycling Route Network 'Pitching Curiosity' 51

The Gap: Presenting Innovation in a Conventional Manner... 51
    #20   Innovation Guru Turns Boardroom Pleaser.................... 51
    #21   Alice is Not Alice... 52
    #22   Curiouser and Curiouser (cried Alice), Too Surprised to
           Speak Good English.. 53

Boldly Go Where No Man Has Gone Before 54
- #23 From Sacrificial Lamb to Success Story 54
- #24 The Gleicher Formula Sparks Curiosity 55
- #25 Guerrilla Warfare as an Innovative Idea 56
- #26 Humans Are Emotional Beings – Be a Storyteller 58

Cycling Route Network 'Measuring Curiosity' 61
- #27 Formula for Change: Logic and Emotion 61
- #28 Curiosity Killed the Cat, but It Made the Company a Star .. 62

We Do Everything Differently 63
- #29 Miami Vice and a Pirate 63
- #30 The Cinderella Principle: Stop Doing What You've Always Done 65
- #31 Evidence 67

Dreamer or Doer 68
- #32 My Revenge on the 'Hard Workers' 68
- #33 Simultaneously, Two Sides of the Same Coin 69
- #34 Idiot 70

Cycling Route Network 'Approaches to Curiosity' 73
- #35 Engaged Employees 73
- #36 The Art of Listening 73
- #37 Framing and Nudging 74
- #38 Antidote and Competitive Advantage 75
- #39 Outsiders and insiders 77
- #40 The Space Pirate in The Martian: Ten Lessons Learned 78
- #41 All-In and the Tourist Principle 81

Eastern vs. Western Thinking 82
- #42 Eastern vs. Western Thinking 82
- #43 Nouns and Verbs: Go with Alice 84

The Cinderella Principle: Don't Look at Things as They Are 85
- #44 Cinderella 85
- #45 Cinderella and Time 87
- #46 Aha Moment 90
- #47 The Proof of the Pudding 91

Cycling Route Network 'Paradox' 95
- #48 Front-Runners and Rear-Guarders 95
- #49 The Risk Paradox 96

Cycling Route Network 'Promoting Curiosity' 101
First Steps 101
- #50 How to Begin..101
- #51 The Wise Guru and the Business Leader: A Lesson in Curiosity..102
- #52 Attracting and Retaining Talent: The Role of Art and Creativity...106
- #53 Customer Loyalty, Customer-Focused and Customer-Centric..108

Cycling Route Network 'Curiosity as a Necessity' 113
- #54 Curiosity is not a Luxury in the Twilight Twenties 113
- #55 From Solution Selling to Curiosity as a Driver............114
- #56 Sell the Pen..115
- #57 Curiosity as a Powerful Marketing Tool......................117
- #58 Communicating Vessels: Successful Innovation, Marketing, and Profit..118
- #59 The Curious See the Hyperconnected Network Society........119

Cycling Route Network 'Roadblocks Ahead'................123
- #60 Established, Conservative, the Right Balance..........123
- #61 Recommendations..124
- #62 Brakes On? Framing 127

Cycling Route Network 'Is the Light Green, Orange, or Red?' 129
- #63 Three Boxes on a Beach, Part 1...............................129
- #64 Three Boxes on a Beach, Part 2...............................129
- #65 The Three Boxes, Part 3..131
- #66 An Essential Part of the Three-Box Method.............132
- #67 The Realm of Opportunities: The Orange Box..........133
- #68 The Three-Box Method Revisited............................134

Cycling Route Network 'Types of Curiosity' 137
- #69 Curiosity in Flavours with Todd Kashdan 137
- #70 Three Types of Curiosity 138
- #71 Open Perceptual Loops..139

Cycling Route Network 'Red, Orange, and Green Companies'.. 141
- #72 Checklist: Red, Orange, and Green Companies.......141

Cycling Route Network 'Curiosity as Salvation' 145
- #73 What We Don't Know: Wicked Problems 145
- #74 Curiosity to the Rescue 146
- #75 Three Scenarios in the Twilight Zone 147
- #76 No Need to Choose 148
- #77 The Breakthrough 150

Cycling Route Network 'Lost Curiosity' 153
- #78 Curiosity Lost 153

Cycling Route Network 'Curiosity as a KPI' 157
Where is that KPI? 157
- #79 About a KPI, NPS, and NCS 157
- #80 Towards a Net Curiosity Score 159

Refinements 161
- #81 Initial Refinements 161
- #82 Additional Measurement 162
- #83 Three Dimensions 163

Playbook 168
Your Key to Innovation 168
What is the NCS? 168
What is the NCS Matrix? 168
Why Should Your Company Use the NCS Matrix? 168
How Does It Work? 169
Step-by-step 170
Curiosity for Advanced Practitioners 175
What Are the Three Core Questions? 176
Beyond the Innovation Department: Building a Culture Where Curiosity Can Thrive 177
Practical Insights: Creating 'Playtime' for Innovation in Your Business 180

Afterword 185
Innovation at Sea 185
Why the Boardroom Keeps Passing the Buck 185
The Beatles Didn't Need an Innovation Department .. 186
Corporate Fear of Vulnerability: Where Creativity goes to Die 187
'You Never Give Me Your Money'—The Death of Safe Spaces in Business 187

Let It Be Vulnerable: Why the C-Suite Need to Take Reponsibility 188
The Sgt. Pepper Lesson—No Surveys, Just Vision 188
Diversity, Inclusion, Psychological Safety, and Curiosity... 190
Embracing Curiosity, Diversity, and Inclusion 190
Leaders: How to Supercharge Curiosity 192
How to Foster a Culture of Curiosity 193
The Power of Curiosity in Action 193
The Octopus Brain: A Model for Organisational Flexibility... 194
Why You Should Care About the Octopus Brain Model 195
How Curiosity Fuels the Octopus Brain Model.............. 195
Breaking Down Silos: Curiosity to the Rescue................ 196
A Playbook for Leaders 197

Curiosity: The Antidote to Conservatism. 199
Not Just in Business, But in Politics Too 199
Conservatism's Real Fear: Curiosity 200
But the Future Doesn't Care About Your Control 200
Curiosity as the Antidote 201
Curiostity Is Liberation 202

Final Thoughts..205
The AI Spectre: Scrambled Eggs for Thought 205
AI and Curiosity: The Real Deal 206
Generative AI: The Remix Artist of the Future.................207
The Logic of Lions and the Wonder of Why 207
Finally: The Last Raindrop..209

A Word of Thanks..213

Foreword

> *The cure for boredom is curiosity. There is no cure for curiosity.*

Welcome! You've picked up this book, and here you are, reading it – exactly what I hoped would happen. You started with the word 'welcome', and now look at you – already more than 30 words deep on the first page! Pretty soon, you'll be flipping through pages two, three, and four. If I've done my job right, you'll keep going, curiosity in full gear, all the way to the very last word. And trust me, that final word isn't what you expect in a business book.

Now, chances are you've just skipped ahead to check out that last word (go ahead, I won't judge). And when you did, you probably thought, "Huh, that was unexpected." If you haven't done it yet, don't worry, you might still. That's curiosity at work. And that's exactly the point – there's no rule saying you need to read this book from page 1 to page 2 to page 3. You can do that, of course, but if you feel like jumping around, be my guest. Curiosity is your guide.

I had a blast writing this book about the Net Curiosity Score (NCS). That wasn't always the case with my other writing projects. My first book? That was pure torture. I've always loved playing with language and writing short pieces. But a book? That's a whole different beast, and taming it was tough. It turns out a book needs structure and chapters – things my brain doesn't naturally do. It was like trying to fit my wild, bubbling thoughts into neat little boxes. Painful. (By the way, I'll explain later why what looks like chaos in my head isn't actually chaos at all. Stick around for that.)

Now, let me tell you what I do instead – keynotes. I've done over 1,600 of them. Easy, no pain, and structured. But here's the thing: keynotes and books? Totally different animals. A keynote is like a short story, a blog post, or a LinkedIn article. I can whip one up without breaking a sweat. Plus, every keynote is unique, shaped by the audience and the moment. In a talk, I can make mental leaps that wouldn't work in a book. And, I get to tweak a keynote endlessly – it's never really finished. A book, though? It's locked in place. Once it's done, it's done.

Bicycle Route Network 'Route Planner'

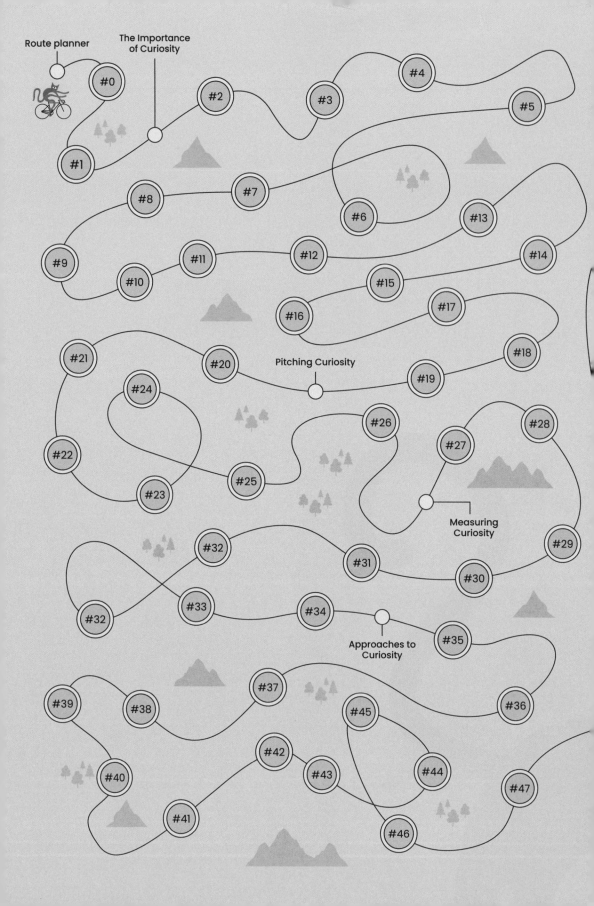

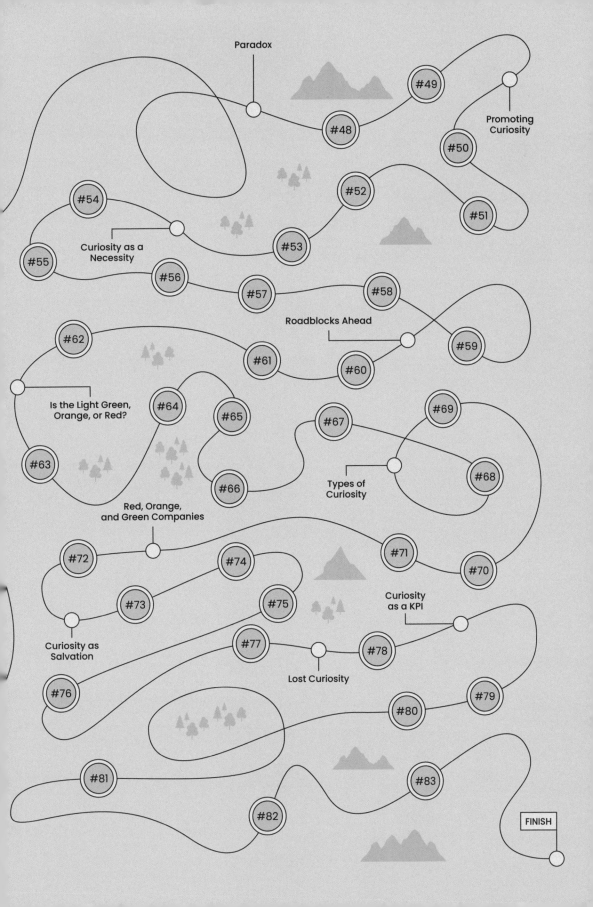

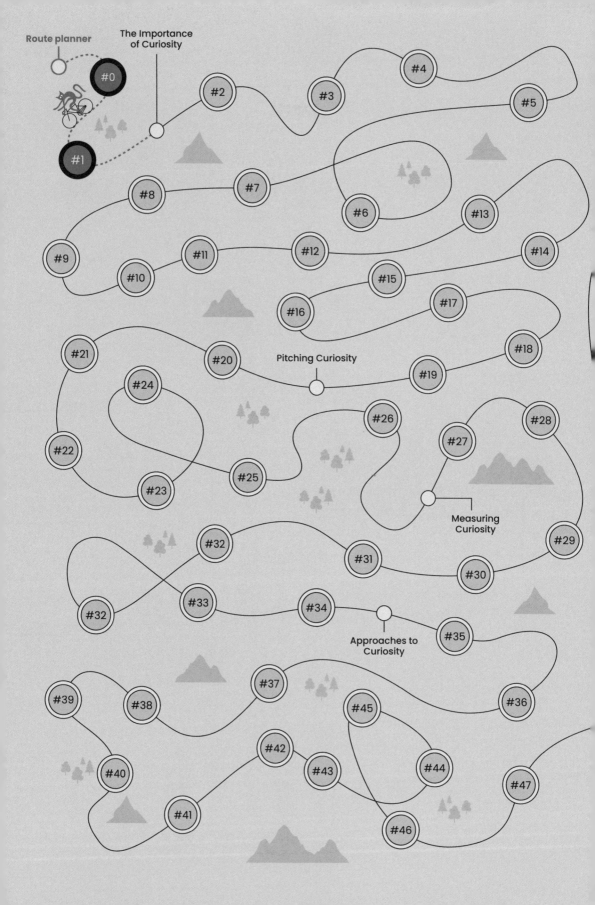

Bicycle Route Network 'Route Planner'

#0 Cycling Junctions

At the start of 2024, I decided to ditch the traditional chapter format and write this book as one continuous flow, from start to finish. Naturally, this gave my publisher a minor heart attack. So, to prevent a meltdown, I came up with a compromise – a structure that balances my chaotic brain (and let's be real, reality itself) with the order that a book demands. After a bit of awkward fumbling – I'm not exactly great at explaining these things – I wrote to my publisher about my brilliant idea.

What's this delightful plan, you ask? Well, it's a book you can read however you like: front to back, skipping around, or – wait for it – **through a network of 'junctions'**, just like the cycling routes that crisscross the Netherlands and Belgium. These bike networks let you pick your own path, hopping from junction to junction, creating your own adventure. At each intersection, you'll find a numbered sign pointing the way. You decide which junctions to follow and in what order, choosing the length and scenery of your ride.

As you can see from this book, the publisher agreed to my plan (probably after a lot of deep breathing).

→#1

#1 *Mulholland Drive* and *The OA*

Once I committed to writing the way I think – in short bursts, like pebbles dropped into your stream of consciousness, causing ripples – I started justifying this approach to myself. It's what we humans do, right? Rationalise our crazy ideas. What I'm trying to do with this book (and I think I'm succeeding) is show you how curiosity influences everything: creativity, innovation, resilience, adaptability, leadership, organisational culture, marketing, sales, and yes, even profitability. This format fits that goal perfectly.

Here's why:

1. *Accessibility*. Short chunks of text that fit into the busiest schedules. You can read a quick piece during a coffee break or on your commute. I'm not stealing your time, I'm filling in the gaps.
2. *Engagement*. Curiosity is a powerful motivator. Each section is a fragment of the larger puzzle, and as you put the pieces together, your curiosity will pull you along.
3. *Diversity of Perspectives*. I get to jump around and offer different angles on curiosity, creativity, and innovation. This isn't a one-size-fits-all business book. There's something here for everyone.
4. *Cohesion*. While each piece stands on its own, they all come together to form a bigger picture. It's your job to connect the dots and create that picture.
5. *Different*. Let's face it – this book is different. It pushes the boundaries, steps beyond them, and dares to challenge the usual business book format.

I'm a huge fan of the movie *Mulholland Drive* and the Netflix series *The OA* – both brilliant, both maddening. Neither follows a conventional storyline. I've watched *Mulholland Drive* over 70 times (well, it feels like it), and I still don't fully get it. Eventually, I realised the movie only makes sense when you stop trying to 'watch' it and instead become a co-creator. It's uncomfortable, and I love that. *The OA*? Same deal. The series doesn't let you sit back and relax – it messes with your brain, breaking every TV rule there is. Episodes vary wildly in length, the plot makes zero sense at times, and yet it keeps you hooked.

When I thought about how to pull you, the reader, out of your comfort zone while keeping things manageable, the idea hit me: cycling junctions.

→#0

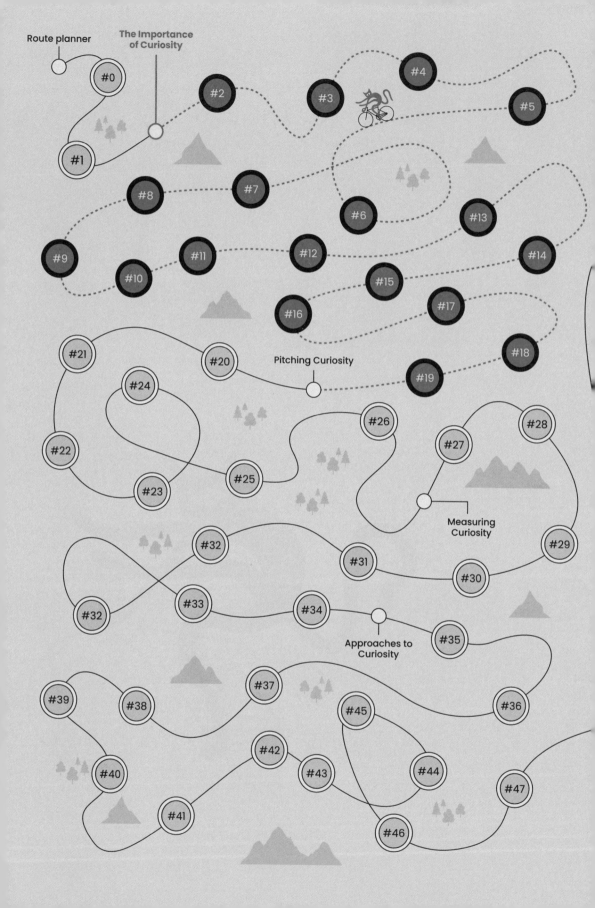

Cycling Route Network 'The Importance of Curiosity'

Route *Alice in Wonderland*

#2 Boosting Curiosity is Boosting Profitability

I often find myself in unfamiliar cities, and I have a routine. When possible, I like to leave the hotel early in the morning with no map, no plan, and no destination. I just wander. I always discover something. Sometimes it's a spark of inspiration, an interesting photo, or a conversation with a stranger in a bookstore (who gifts you *Atlas Shrugged* and claims their name is Alice) → #21. Other times, I stumble upon a hidden museum where I can enjoy a Turner or Rothko in near solitude. Or, I turn a corner and find myself face-to-face with a breathtaking cathedral.

These discoveries feel far more meaningful than anything I'd find on a guided tour. I stumble onto things that make me think, "I can use this later." I don't always know how or when, but the ideas always find a place – whether in a book, a keynote, or a random LinkedIn post. One morning in London, I spotted an old edition of *Alice in Wonderland* in a shop window. The shop was closed, and I couldn't return after my talk, so I bought a copy online later. Little did I know, *Alice in Wonderland* is actually about our VUCA world – Volatile, Uncertain, Complex, and Ambiguous. In this world, we're all Alice.

The Cheshire Cat summed it up best:

[
If you don't know where you're going, any road will get you there.
]

Many people think this means you should have a clear goal, but in business, goals can be meaningless in a world as unpredictable as Wonderland. The cat might actually be telling us to embrace the journey and discover our goals along the way.

I started collecting different editions of *Alice in Wonderland* after that. There's something magical about wandering without a plan, discovering new places, and finding unexpected treasures. Maybe that's why I named my orange MPV The Curiosity Mobile. It's my partner in crime on many of these discovery trips. The name also nods to the book you're now holding, which I was still writing at the time. But now it's done. You're holding a business book about curiosity, magic, and imagination – words that most people in 'serious' business frown at. Curiosity is seen as child's play, right? Well, guess what? I promise you this book will show you that curiosity is directly linked to innovation, agility, and future-proofing your organisation. And yes, curiosity boosts profitability. Curious now?

→ #3

> *Boosting curiosity is boosting profitability.*

#3 A Life in Lyrics

On a cold, clear morning in late February 2024, I found myself cruising in my trusty orange Curiosity Mobile toward a château near Paris. My mission? To lead a full-day session for the London Business School on one of my favourite topics: the power of curiosity in business. My goal was simple: spark a curiosity fire in the participants, something that would burn bright not just during the session but long after, in their work and real lives. For years, I'd been writing about this idea and lecturing on it, but now it was all coming together in this book – centreed around a concept I'd developed mostly during the Covid-19 pandemic: the Net Curiosity Score (NCS). The NCS is a way to measure and boost curiosity in both people and organisations. And why does that matter? Because doing so improves everything – innovation, customer service, marketing, company culture, creativity, and ultimately, profitability.

As I drove along the quiet highway between Lille and Paris, I hit play on a podcast I'd recently discovered: *A Life in Lyrics*. It's a series of conversations with Sir Paul McCartney (half of the greatest songwriting duo ever, if you ask me), where he tells the stories behind some of his songs. McCartney's warm, Liverpool-accented voice filled the car as he talked about *The Magical Mystery Tour*. He explained that he wrote the song to capture the childlike curiosity he had while wandering around Liverpool, discovering new things just for the joy of it.

Listening to him talk about wandering without a clear destination, trusting that something interesting would happen, hit me hard. That's the kind of curiosity I love. The kind where you're not aiming for anything specific, you're just exploring because you can. It's not aimless

– it's adventurous. And yes, I know that some people reading this might already be tempted to close the book because businesses are all about goals, right? But hear me out.

We've been told for over a century that goals are everything. We've created this dictatorship of objectives, where not having a clear goal is seen as failure. But the truth is, goals can limit us, especially in a world that's changing faster than ever. There's value in Adventurous Curiosity, which might sound less intimidating than 'aimless curiosity'. More on that later.

←#3 →#4

#4 Roll Up, Roll Up

I like to call Adventurous Curiosity the *Alice in Wonderland* Curiosity.

> *If you don't know where you're going,*
> *any road will get you there.*

This is exactly the kind of curiosity that leads you to discoveries you didn't even know you were looking for. What might happen along the way? Pure magic. In the business world, they call that game-changing innovation. It's the kind of breakthrough that happens when you step outside the comfort zone of the known and venture into the unknown. It's why companies need to act like a disobedient child sometimes – going beyond what's allowed, exploring the exciting, the dangerous, the risky.

As I drove toward the château near Paris for my session with the London Business School (see #3), I rolled down my window to grab a ticket at the French Péage. I couldn't help but smile because I knew that what I'd just been thinking was a bit like heresy in the church of traditional management. But I knew I'd write this down later, and that you, the reader, would come across it eventually. How would it feel? Probably a bit provocative, maybe a little unsettling. Perfect, I thought. But don't worry. Alice in Wonderland Curiosity is just one kind of curiosity. There's another that businesses are much more familiar with: goal-oriented curiosity. This is the kind where you have a clear objective and you work out how to get there. You draw on all your knowledge and skills, and those who have been the most explorative in their curiosity have the biggest toolbox to succeed. Take *The Martian* as an example (we'll get to that later – see #40). The protagonist, stranded on Mars, has to use his knowledge of botany to survive. He never thought his expertise would be useful for something like that, but his curiosity and ability to problem-solve saved him.

Companies need to embrace both adventurous and goal-oriented curiosity. Not only because adventurous curiosity is the engine of real, groundbreaking innovation, but because both types feed each other. Without exploratory curiosity, there are no bold goals. Without challenging goals, there's no goal-oriented curiosity to solve problems. And without innovation, a company stands still. And standing still is death in business.

The podcast (see #3) went on, and I learned that the real *Magical Mystery Tour* from McCartney's childhood wasn't magical or mysterious at all. It was a predictable, touristy bus trip to a fairground attraction on the English coast. And here's what hit me: that predictability is exactly what companies love. They cling to what they know, to control, to the safety of the known. "Curiosity killed the cat," they say. In the world of business, adventurous, aimless curiosity is seen as a distraction, something dangerous. Why venture into the unknown when what you have works just fine?

But here's the thing: a silent killer doesn't always knock on the front door. Sometimes, it slips through the cracks. And only aimless curiosity can reveal those cracks in time. That's why I'm writing this book about the Net Curiosity Score (NCS): to show business leaders that curiosity – every form of it – is probably the most overlooked and powerful tool in business today. It's time to start measuring it, nurturing it, and, most importantly, using it.

So hop on that *Magical Mystery Tour* bus, I thought, as I kept driving. No one could hear me, so no one could call me crazy. I glanced at my GPS and saw I still had some distance to go before I reached Château Fillerval near Paris, where I'd be teaching that day. I hadn't been there before, and I didn't know the participants. That feeling of excitement bubbled up again. I turned up the volume and sang along with The Beatles:

> *Roll up, roll up for the mystery tour. The magical mystery tour is waiting to take you away. Waiting to take you away. Take you today.*

←#3 #2 →#5

#5 Parallel World

The business world is a parallel universe. Let me explain. I often like to stir things up a bit by telling people they need to read *Alice in Wonderland*. Why? Because they are Alice in Wonderland. The simple explanation is that we live in a VUCA world – volatile, uncertain, complex, and ambiguous (see #2). But there's a deeper layer to it. What most business leaders don't realise is that they've created their own Wonderland. It looks like the real world, but it isn't. It's a bubble with its own rules. Rules that don't necessarily apply outside of their carefully crafted bubble.

Are you still with me? Good. It's like a dream within a dream – a Wonderland within Wonderland.

I spent years in the corporate world, and let me tell you, it's a world unto itself. I never really felt at home there. Maybe I survived because I approached it with a childlike sense of curiosity. I observed, much like a child watches adults, trying to make sense of it all. Curiosity was my flashlight. But at the same time, I had to be careful. I had to pretend I understood everything while secretly questioning it all.

Curiosity didn't just help me think; it helped me rethink things. That's how I earned a reputation for 'thinking innovatively'. But here's the catch: not everyone saw that as a good thing. Quite the opposite. To some, I was a loose cannon, a dreamer, a threat to the comfortable, controlled world they'd built. Curiosity was my ally, but because it was viewed as the enemy, I had to keep it hidden. Friends of the enemy, after all, are also enemies. Looking back, writing this book about curiosity and its value to businesses feels like sweet revenge. For years, I had to hide this superpower, only daring to use it in secret. Curiosity was seen as inappropriate in the business world, especially back in the 1990s and early 2000s. I hope this book isn't just a personal liberation; I hope it's a victory for curiosity, turning it into a KPI that every business values. Fifteen years after stepping out of that corporate bubble, I don't need to prove anything. I can't go back and say, "See? I was right all along." But I can show where companies stand now, how leadership has evolved, and why curiosity is no longer a luxury but a necessity. My goal? To help businesses and leaders break free from their fear of curiosity. As children, we learn by being curious. We explore because we want to know more, and that's the only reward we need. But somewhere along the way, we lose that curiosity. We stop learning for the sake of learning and start doing it for rewards – grades, diplomas, promotions. That's where we go wrong. That's what this book is here to fix.

←#4#3#2 →#6

#6 Chernobyl Syndrome or Conscious Blindness

I vividly remember watching the first episode of HBO's *Chernobyl* during a long flight from San Francisco to Europe. It was brilliantly crafted, dark, and horrifying all at once. My in-flight meal? Completely unappetising. I felt like I could taste the metallic air of 1986, where everything went tragically wrong in the USSR. By the time I finished the episode, I knew I had to watch it again. It was a perfect metaphor for how companies handle inconvenient realities: they ignore and deny them, only to make the fallout far worse.

Soon after, I wrote a piece about it and started using the concept in my keynotes. I call it the Chernobyl Syndrome. Now, you've probably heard of the China Syndrome, the catastrophic (and thankfully fictional) scenario where a nuclear meltdown bores a hole right through the Earth. But the Chernobyl Syndrome isn't a physical phenomenon; it's a mindset. And unfortunately, it's real. It's the way companies can become willfully blind to the truth, mistaking their internal bubble of 'order' for the actual reality outside. Even when the gap between those two worlds becomes dangerously wide.

I watched that episode a third time. I saw the denial in the control room, the assumptions that were made, and the moment when a concerned observer was dismissed with those chilling words: "Get him out of here, he's delusional." I've heard variations of that phrase in real-life business settings too many times. Sitting on that plane, I couldn't stop thinking about why companies become their own worst enemies. What could the antidote be? The answer hit me: curiosity. Curiosity could have changed everything in that control room. Instead of dismissing the observer, a healthy dose of curiosity might have prompted questions, investigations, and – most importantly – solutions. At that point, my obsession with curiosity was no longer surprising to me. It was becoming obvious that curiosity was the driving force behind creativity, innovation, and growth. I kept writing, and I kept telling people: the book is coming.

←#5#4#3#2 →#7

#7 Bitterballen and Buttermilk, My New Content

In 2015, Microsoft Netherlands asked me to help them organise an event focused on customer-centric business practices. I had just entered the world of professional keynote speaking, and I suggested bringing in two heavyweights: Peter Hinssen and Steven Van Belleghem. The idea was to have three Belgians (us) on stage in Bussum, Netherlands, inspiring Dutch entrepreneurs about technology. A few weeks after that initial conversation, Nexxworks was born, and I became its CEO.

Now, Peter and Steven are giants in the field, so I knew I needed to bring something new to the table. Our topics naturally overlapped, and the last thing I wanted was to sound like an echo of their ideas. My solution? Create new content that would set my keynote apart. And I needed a strong visual anchor for the whole thing.

I found that anchor in the most unexpected way – on social media.

The event was called Microsoft Customer Engagement 2015. In early April, I came across a headline that stopped me in my tracks: "Jamie Dimon: I lay awake at night." Intrigued (and aware that clickbait was alive and well), I dove into the article. Dimon, CEO of JP Morgan Chase, had just published his annual letter to shareholders. The headline that grabbed me the most? "The startups in Silicon Valley are eating Wall Street's lunch."

And with that, I had my opening line for the keynote, along with a joke: "Peter, Steven, and I come from Belgium, where lunch is a bit more than bitterballen and buttermilk, and stealing each other's lunch is a serious crime." Corny? Yes. But in the Netherlands, a little charm and a Flemish accent go a long way. As I read the article, the narrative unfolded effortlessly. Jamie Dimon admitted that the bank had made three huge mistakes:

1. Underestimating the impact of technology on society.
2. Losing sight of the customer by focusing too much on internal processes.
3. Being caught off guard by the speed of change.

That was all I needed. Dimon's conclusion was clear: as the world around them changed, JP Morgan Chase had gotten too comfortable, too focused on themselves, and had left a gap in the market. Startups, of course, were more than happy to fill that gap.

And then came the quote I knew I could use to drive my point home:

> *Maybe people will still do banking, but the question is: will they still need banks?*

That single line encapsulated everything I needed for my keynote. Dimon himself was acknowledging that their failure to stay curious, to innovate, and to focus on the customer had created the very market conditions where tech companies could flourish. It was a gift. I built my keynote around that theme and delivered it with fresh energy. And yes, the bitterballen and buttermilk joke? It landed just as well as I'd hoped.

←#6#5#4#3#2 →#8

Curiosity or a Tsunami Ambush?

#8 Beach Chair Syndrome

I was sitting alone at a hotel near Schiphol, eating dinner with my trusty tablet propped up against the salt and pepper shakers. That evening's meal? Vegetarian risotto – healthy and, more importantly, easy to eat with one hand while swiping with the other. It's a whole technique, really. I was re-reading the article about James Dimon (see #7), bouncing in my seat because I had finally found my story for the Microsoft Customer Engagement event. Eureka! Back in my hotel room later that night, with planes roaring overhead, I started building my keynote slides. The story flowed, but I still hadn't cracked the key piece: the image. You know, the one that would make everyone sit up straight and think, "Ah, I get it." I needed an image that clearly screamed, "Stop fiddling with your internal processes and start looking outwards. And fast."

The next morning at breakfast, the image still hadn't come to me, and the event was approaching. Espresso, croissant, Dutch cheese – no inspiration. But then, while re-reading that article for the third time, I saw it:

[*We saw the digital tsunami too late.*]

I suddenly knew what I needed. The missing image, the metaphor, the story I'd been searching for all night flashed in front of me: The Beach Chair Syndrome. Here's the idea: Jamie Dimon and many CEOs like him had been sitting on the beach for 20 years, watching the digital wave slowly form. And yet, when it finally crashed down, they still claimed, "We saw it too late." Really? How can you miss something that had been building for two decades? Enter The Beach Chair Syndrome.

The image I wanted was an aerial view of a crowded beach, rows and rows of coloured beach chairs packed together by rental companies. Red, blue, yellow – all clustered in their little territories, fighting for market share. It's the same story with businesses: markets get overcrowded, and companies get stuck fighting over tiny slices of the pie. I searched for hours but couldn't find the right image. Even today, with tools like DALL-E, I still can't quite capture what I'm after. But the metaphor stuck – and became one of the cornerstones of my keynotes ever since. Nine years later, it led to this book. A very long pregnancy, indeed.

←#7#6#5#4#3#2 →#9

#9 Towering Wave of Resistance to Change

Imagine this scenario, I tell the audience at the event: you're running a beach chair business. You rent them out on a crowded beach. You've got fierce competition – other rental companies right next to you. What do you do all day? You're busy fighting for market share. You inch forward, steal a bit of territory from your neighbour on the left, hoping the one on the right doesn't steal yours. It's a constant battle. And besides that, you focus on operational excellence – doing the same thing, but better, sharper, faster.

But while you're fighting for space on the beach and optimising those beach chairs, something's brewing in the distance. Jamie Dimon's statement, *"We saw the digital tsunami too late,"* paints the picture perfectly.

CEOs like him were so focused on the beach and the competition that they missed the swelling wave of change behind them. And this is where it gets interesting. I pause during my talk and let the audience reflect on it. The digital wave had been rising for decades – search engines, social media, e-commerce, the platform economy. But Dimon's team didn't look up. They were too busy burying their heads in the sand, optimising processes and focusing on operational excellence.

Why? Because humans – especially in business – are naturally resistant to change. We crave stability, tradition, and predictability. We only adapt when forced to, and by then, it's often too late. Businesses are no different. They're led by people who hate risk and lock everything down into management systems and scorecards. They're not programmed to change, and that's why they often miss the big waves.

← #8#7#6#5#4#3#2 → #10

#10 A True 4000 Holes: Measuring for the Sake of Measuring

Now, picture this: the digital tsunami is on its way, I tell the audience. What happens when a tsunami approaches? The beach gets wider – a lot wider. And what do businesses do when the beach suddenly expands? They double down. Heads down, they start placing more beach chairs as fast as possible. Competitors are doing the same, so everyone's hustling to grab more ground before the tide comes back in. Sound familiar?

I reenact this frantic scene on stage, hauling imaginary beach chairs while the audience becomes the ocean. This is what companies do – keep themselves busy, busy, busy. They measure everything. KPIs, scorecards, metrics – counting for the sake of counting.

> *I read the news today, oh boy*
> *Four thousand holes in Blackburn, Lancashire*
> *And though the holes were rather small*
> *They had to count them all*
> *Now they know how many holes it takes*
> *to fill the Albert Hall.*

You see the wave coming – maybe someone even nudges you and says, "Hey, take a look at that out there." But you shrug it off. It's just a small wave, right? Nothing to worry about. You're too busy placing chairs, beating the competition, optimising your processes. Business as usual. And then, suddenly, the wave hits. Jamie Dimon realises too late that the chairs he's been fighting to place on the beach don't matter anymore. They're washed away in an instant, along with everything he thought was so urgent. I let that image sink in – pun intended – and then ask the audience: What did Jamie do wrong? And how could curiosity have saved him?

←#9#8#7#6#5#4#3#2 →#11

#11 Porter's Five as Kindling

So, what went wrong at JP Morgan Chase in 2015? Well, the issue had been brewing long before that year, but in 2015, it became glaringly obvious: the bank was so focused on managing itself that it completely missed the signals from the outside world. It's not a rare problem. This is the Chernobyl Syndrome all over again (see #6). They simplified the outside world into a few convenient assumptions and lost touch with reality. It's like being on the beach and seeing the tide go out. You notice that the beach is suddenly much wider, but you chalk it up to just another low tide – nothing unusual. Maybe you even order a few more beach chairs from China to capitalise on the extra space. And when you spot a strange wave on the horizon, you shrug it off because, well, there are always waves, right? This is how businesses operate. They rely on assumptions. And when those assumptions go unchallenged, they become dangerous.

Jamie Dimon's team was used to battling other banks. The battlefield was familiar, and so were the competitors. But when new players entered the field with digital superpowers, suddenly the whole game changed. It wasn't just the competitors that were different – the battlefield itself had shifted. New laws of nature seemed to apply. And to make things worse, the new competitors weren't just a few – they were hundreds, all with different tactics and weapons. It's no wonder Jamie was losing sleep. What Jamie was really saying, without quite saying it, was this: Porter's Five Forces – the holy grail of business strategy – was now kindling for the fire. The old rules no longer applied. Newcomers weren't playing by the same game. They went digital. They used new tools, while the traditional companies had no idea how to adapt.

←#10#9#8#7#6#5#4#3#2 →#12

#12 Cars on the Beach or Standing on the Surfboard

Some companies aren't just setting up beach chairs – they're heading out into the open ocean, searching for the next big wave. From the beach, these waves look like tsunamis, terrifying and destructive. But for the companies out in the water? It's thrilling. The bigger the wave, the better the surf. Of course, no one starts out surfing those giant waves. It takes practice. You learn to surf by surfing, and sometimes, a wave grows faster than you can ride it. Sometimes, a promising wave fizzles out. But real surfers always look for the next wave, knowing that the magic happens in the open water, not on the beach.

Here's the catch: you can't ride a wave from the shore. If you spend all your time on the beach, no matter how well you optimise your beach chair business, you're going to get wiped out when the wave hits. Take the automotive industry as an example. It's been a tsunami waiting to happen for years, and I've been using it as a warning since my first book in 2017. The boundaries between industries – automotive, technology, entertainment, energy – are blurring. The entire mobility world is being rewritten. What's happening to the automotive industry could happen to any industry tomorrow.

←#11#10#9#8#7#6#5#4#3#2 →#13

#13 Heading Out to the Open Ocean – Because You Must

Now, I know what you're thinking: "I can't just float around on a surfboard all day, waiting for waves. I'll starve!" And you're right. You don't need to spend all your time in the open ocean. There's nothing wrong with running your beach chair business. In fact, it's essential. But you must take time to venture out into the water – away from the beach and your daily operations – to feel the waves forming. You might be thinking, "Can't I just stay on the beach and observe the ocean from there?" Sure, you can try. But here's why it doesn't work:

1. You're too close to your beach chairs. You'll keep one eye on the beach, and even if you think you're observing the waves, you're not fully engaged. Your mind is still wrapped up in daily concerns.
2. You can't feel the waves from the shore. You need to be out there, in the water, to truly understand which waves are growing and which aren't.
3. If a wave grows quickly, you'll be on the wrong side of it. Trying to ride a wave from the beach is a losing game. It's too late.
4. A giant wave blocks your view of what's beyond it. If you're focused on the massive wave rushing toward you, you'll miss everything else happening further out in the ocean. You'll be stuck reacting instead of anticipating.

So no, staying on the beach and observing isn't enough. You need to head out into the ocean now and then, feel the waves growing, and decide which ones you can't afford to miss. Normally, I'm not a fan of saying you must do something, but this is one of those times. You must leave the beach.

←#12#11#10#9#8#7#6#5#4#3#2 →#14

Houston, we have a problem

#14 Outside Your and My Comfort Zone

In 2016, I had the opportunity to teach for the first time at the London Business School. However, this wasn't in London. On a Sunday, I flew to Geneva and then took the train along Lake Geneva, passing through Lausanne and finally arriving in Vevey, Switzerland. I stayed in a cosy Swiss hotel with a view of the lake and the imposing Mont Blanc massif in the background – a mountain with an impressively fitting name. The next day, I walked about 500 metres to the Nestlé training centre, as Nestlé was London Business School's client. I taught for a full day to a group of around 60 managers. The assignment was clear: prepare them for the future. Back then, the session consisted of two blocks of three hours each, filled with pure lecturing. Nowadays, I approach it very differently – much more interactivly. One-to-many has become much more of a many-to-many dynamic. Central authority and purely one-way communication have given way to the enriching effect of two-way dialogue and distributed authority. My transformation is tied to three key elements. The most significant is that, after years of working with innovation, technology, customer-centric thinking, leadership, and culture, I feel so at home with the content that I'm now willing to engage openly and expose myself to all kinds of questions, challenges, and counterarguments. Back in 2016, I was immensely proud and honoured to give it a try for such a prestigious institution. I had never dreamed of it, and I assumed it would be a few sessions at most. Little did I know that I would end up delivering over 250 sessions for London Business School, for a diverse range of clients like Randstad, FrieslandCampina, Nestlé, Vodafone, TCS, Dell, Continental, Coca-Cola, Valeo, and Engie.

Another shift came from a "Houston, we have a problem" phone call from London Business School, sometime before the summer of 2017. My sessions in Vevey had become an issue. In my view, they were only getting better, as I was increasingly challenging the status quo and pushing the attending leaders out of their comfort zones, sparking their curiosity about what lay 'out there' and what the future held. Participant scores kept rising, yet there was a problem: frustration among managers who felt limited in how much they could translate their newfound knowledge and enthusiasm into action. Senior management felt uneasy about this. A gap had developed between the organisation's status quo and the forward drive of the participants after my sessions. I was, in a way, doing my job too well. There were two options: tone it down (the school's preferred option) or not (my preferred option). I firmly stated that the problem didn't lie with me or my content, but with the company, which wanted to work towards the future, but only so far. I suggested an interactive workshop for the senior leadership, co-created with the school, to let them experience the thrill of breaking free from the daily grind and to understand its importance for an organisation. I realised that this was anything but a safeIt's not 'anything but an all-or-nothing choice'? It was all-or-nothing? If this had failed, it would have been the end for me – not only with Nestlé but also with the school. Additionally, I acted as if I had a ready-made workshop that I had delivered hundreds of times, but that wasn't true. I still had to create it. In September 2017, I delivered my very first interactive session, using newly designed methods. It was a success. The rest is history. My session has since become a staple in the leadership programme at London Business School, with thousands of current and future leaders actively participating. The third change... well, that remains a surprise for now – or head over to #16 to find out.

← #13 #12 #11 #10 #9 #8 #7 #6 #5 #4 #3 #2   → #15

#15 Defeating the Big Bad Monster

Then, suddenly, in Vevey, at that traditional FMCG company in Switzerland – where people had decades of corporate experience and seemed more rooted in processes than an ancient oak in the forest – I witnessed something extraordinary. Three presentations absolutely blew me away. It was as if these senior managers, who many would dismiss as 'corporate dinosaurs', had suddenly erupted like long-dormant volcanoes. Out came scalding hot ideas, passion, and creativity, unleashed with the kind of enthusiasm you'd expect from fresh-faced 20-somethings. Fireworks – but professional ones. It was that combination of experience and raw creative energy that thrilled me. These senior managers were on fire. We started Nexxworks because we were afraid older European companies would be swept away by the digital tsunami (see #8). That fear still exists. But in Vevey, I saw hope.

The hope didn't come from startups, young disruptors, or flashy tech firms – it came from these seasoned professionals, people often dismissed as out of touch. I saw sparks of brilliance. But with those sparks came the fear: the Big Bad Nameless Monster that stalks the corridors of large enterprises. You know it – the one that suffocates innovation and crushes new ideas. These managers feared it too. They worried that their nearly miraculous ideas would remain just that – ideas, with no path to execution.

The true battle wasn't about having great ideas – it was about transforming those ideas into action, into experiments that could scale and truly change the company. The lesson? Present these same managers with a fresh idea tomorrow, and they'll view it through the same old corporate lens, reshaping it until it's no longer innovative. But when they generate those ideas themselves, everything changes. Suddenly, they think in new patterns, break old metrics, and dare to be creative. And they absolutely can be.

←#14#13#12#11#10#9#8#7#6#5#4#3#2 →#16

#16 The Third Thing, a Valuable Discovery

If you've been paying attention, you probably noticed in #14 that I only covered two out of the three reasons for becoming more interactive. Now it's time for the third, and it has everything to do with curiosity

– the heart of this book. After my success in Vevey, I wrote excitedly to the London Business School about the experience. The response was formal but insightful:

"It sounds like you've made a valuable discovery in your approach. Transforming your keynotes into interactive sessions centreed around curiosity has not only increased engagement but also fostered a mutual learning environment. By being curious about your audience's curiosity, you've created a dynamic space where knowledge is exchanged, and everyone, including yourself, learns more. This beautifully illustrates how curiosity can lead to deeper insights and more meaningful experiences for all involved."

That was the lightbulb moment: curiosity. My previous long keynotes – where I delivered my knowledge to a passive audience – lacked that spark. I was so focused on dumping information that I missed the interaction. It was a one-way street. Through that first workshop in Vevey, I discovered that by being curious about my audience's curiosity, I could create a much more dynamic learning experience. The energy in the room shifted. People weren't just absorbing – they were engaging.

Curiosity, I realised, isn't just about acquiring knowledge – it's a catalyst for faster and deeper learning. My sessions became less about me talking and more about facilitating curiosity, and everyone in the room benefited, myself included.

←#15#14#13#12#11#10#9#8#7#6#5#4#3#2 →#17

#17 Superpower, the Child Awakens

I've shared my experiences in routes #14 to #16 for two reasons. First, they represent pivotal moments in the last decade that nudged me toward writing this book. Second, they tie into one of the workshops that's now a staple at London Business School: the Superpower/Kryptonite exercise.

Picture this: 50 top executives from one of the world's largest companies, gathered in a room overlooking Lake Geneva. Grey hair, grey suits, white shirts, red ties, and blue blazers. These senior leaders were there with me, diving into big data, AI (yes, even back in 2017), and the rapidly changing world. I challenged them to think about how they'd stay relevant beyond 2030, which – at the time – seemed distant, far beyond their active careers. During a break, we took a short walk outside. One senior leader put his arm around me, pointed to the serene lake and mountains, and said with a chuckle, "Is it any wonder we don't see the changing world from here?" I couldn't have said it better myself.

Later, I introduced the Superpower/Kryptonite workshop. I divided the executives into five groups and challenged them to outdo. Their task?

1. A Superpower. What unique strength would make them unbeatable against the other groups?
2. Kryptonite. What would be their Achilles' heel? What weakness would leave them vulnerable?

As I explained the challenge, I had a little voice in my head saying, "Rik, can you really pull this off with these top execs?" But I pressed on. And to my surprise, they dove in wholeheartedly. Maybe it was the drive to win, or maybe I was waking the child inside them, bit by bit. The reason I keep doing this workshop is simple: the definition of leadership today is about developing your company's superpowers and eliminating the kryptonite that's holding you back. In 2017, one group came up with a memorable duo:

> *Passionate Curiosity is our SuperPower*
> *and complete lack of Curiosity is the Kryptonite*
> *we give the others.*

←#16#15#14#13#12#11#10#9#8#7#6#5#4#3#2 →#18

#18 Gentle Bell Curves vs. Shark Fins: Tsunamis in Wonderland

In many of my keynotes on innovation, I often refer to a diagram from my first book, *Managers The Day After Tomorrow*. It's perfect for explaining the rapid emergence of a tsunami and how quickly it can obliterate industries: the Shark-Fin Curve, in contrast to the familiar bell-shaped Gauss curve of innovation. I first came across this concept in *Big Bang Disruption: Strategy in the Age of Devastating Innovation* by Larry Downes and Paul Nunes. Their book describes a new form of disruption that doesn't follow the classic model, where something new starts slowly, grows gradually, and is only better in quality or price after a while. No, this new type of innovation is better on all fronts from the outset – both cheaper and superior – and it quickly wipes out every segment of the market. In the old world, you had the cosy, predictable Gauss curve. The innovation started slow, had a bit of a rise, and slowly built momentum. The new world? A few tiny ripples signal the beginning of something new, and then suddenly, there's a tipping point – an explosion of change that shoots straight up. The Shark-Fin curve.

Now, I've often used this imagery to highlight the beach chair syndrome (see #8), but when I present this idea, I sometimes encounter resistance, especially from local European companies or even some strategists and professors. They argue it's safer to wait until a new technology or business model matures before getting involved. This tactic of 'wait and see' worked well in the past – wait until the pioneers have paved the way, then swoop in with all your resources and scale faster than they ever could.

But that doesn't work anymore.

Companies used to believe that playing the long game – waiting for the 'right moment' – would allow them to dominate the market with their well-oiled sales and marketing machines. But they missed the fact that the context has changed. When Tesla entered the scene, the traditional automakers thought it was just another passing trend. "Let's wait," they said. "We'll outscale them when the market is ready."

But by the time Tesla's Model 3 dropped in 2018, it was too late. They miscalculated. Twice. First, they realised that innovation wasn't a Gauss curve anymore; it was a tsunami. And trying to jump onto a train that's moving at the speed of light? That only results in bruises and broken bones. The traditional automakers were forced to scramble – making frantic, expensive, and panicked moves to catch up.

Second, while they were focused on the Tesla wave, a much bigger tsunami from the East was already forming. Chinese companies like BYD and NIO weren't just playing catch-up – they were leapfrogging the competition. I even created a T-shirt for my keynotes with an illustration of a small boat, where people are celebrating surviving the first big wave, all while missing the bigger wave approaching behind them. In 2024, traditional car brands are stuck in Alice's Wonderland. They see the world as it once was, not as it is now, and they're missing the new laws of innovation. In Wonderland, waves don't just come from the same direction. They come from all sides, and if you don't see them, you'll get washed away.

> *The key to survival? Curiosity.*

← #17 #16 #15 #14 #13 #12 #11 #10 #9 #8 #7 #6 #5 #4 #3 #2 → #19

#19 Advanced Tightrope Walking: No Risk = The Biggest Risk

We all know it: curiosity is the catalyst for progress, innovation, and renewal. It's the superpower that challenges our ingrained assumptions, making us dream of something bigger, better, or entirely different. And yet, despite all this, why do companies fear curiosity? Why are they scared of the one thing that could save them? Every time I talk about curiosity, I see the light bulbs go off in the audience. They nod along. They get it. They know that curiosity drives innovation – that it's the only way to create a market rather than wait for one. And still, when the rubber hits the road, companies shrink back. Why? Because curiosity leads into uncharted territory, and that means risk. And businesses are trained to avoid risk like it's kryptonite (more on that later). In all my years of exploring business literature, I rarely, if ever, found much mention of curiosity. Instead, I found pages and pages on how to mitigate or avoid risk. As if risk is the great enemy of business. Here's the irony: not taking risks is the biggest risk of all.

> *Not wanting to take any risks is the greatest risk of all.*

Companies get caught in the trap of waiting for a business case. "Is there a proven market for it?" "Show me the numbers first." The result? They stay stuck in their comfort zones, safe and sound, never exploring the wild, unpredictable terrain where real innovation happens. Curiosity requires us to venture into the unknown, to ask "what if?" and "why not?" But most businesses have systems designed to suppress that instinct. It's the kryptonite that keeps them from flying. Leadership today requires an advanced kind of tightrope walking. The balance between fostering curiosity and managing risk isn't easy – it's like trying to keep your footing on a constantly shifting rope. But without curiosity, businesses stagnate. And when that happens, you can forget about innovation.

Curious leaders are better leaders. They create environments where learning and questioning are celebrated. They know that curiosity is the secret sauce that drives everything from product development to sales and marketing. Companies that breathe curiosity don't need to search for customer needs; they naturally find them. At its core, curiosity is the spark that ignites everything. And yet, it's the one thing that gets stifled in the name of 'risk management'. It's time to flip the script.

←#18#17#16#15#14#13#12#11#10#9#8#7#6#5#4#3#2
→Cycling Route Network 'Pitching curiosity'

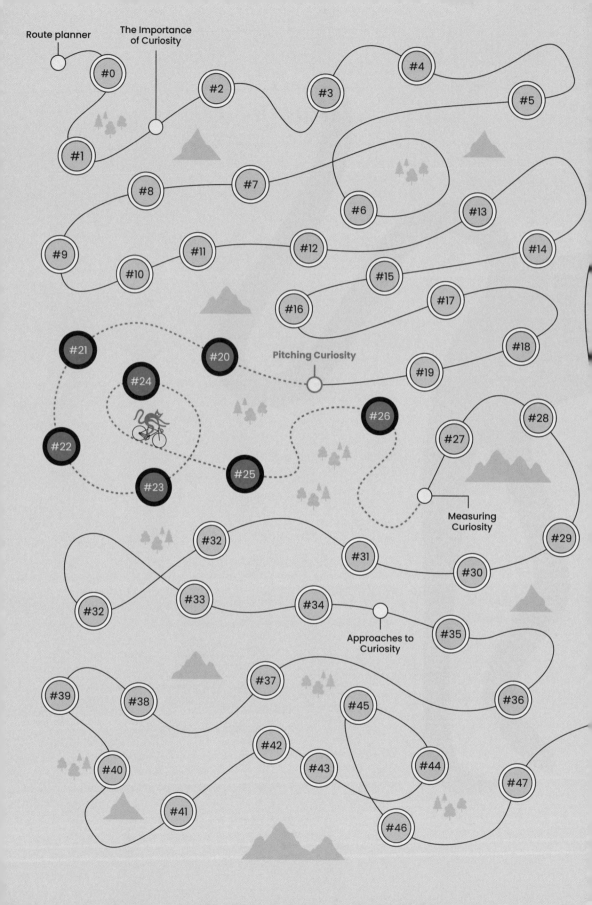

Cycling Route Network 'Pitching Curiosity'

The Gap: Presenting Innovation in a Conventional Manner

#20 Innovation Guru Turns Boardroom Pleaser

Since I started working on this book, I've noticed a disturbing trend: innovation gurus selling out to the corporate world. Take one well-known guru, for instance. He used to be the guy with the wild hair, the eccentric outfits, the kind of guy who'd drop to the floor in a fit of mock agony during his keynotes, railing against the evils of traditional business practices. He'd scream that asking for a business case was the death of innovation, and I agreed with him. Asking for a business case too soon does kill innovation. But now? I see him writing articles that preach the opposite. He advises innovators to behave conservatively, follow the rules, and present their ideas with boring, old-school business cases.

Wait. What?

This is the same guy who used to dance on stage like a rock star of innovation, now telling people to get in line, suit up, and stick to the playbook? What happened to him? Did he sell out? Or has he forgotten the very thing that made him an innovator in the first place? In his article, he says that to succeed in the boardroom, you need to package your wild, disruptive idea in the dullest, most conventional way possible: make a business case, present a strategic plan, and play it safe.

Reading this, I felt like I was being gaslighted. Was this the same guy? Had he lost faith? Or worse, was he just pandering to the executives, trying to worm his way into their innovation departments without rocking the boat too much? Here's the thing: you can't sell innovation by playing it safe. If Mick Jagger had toned down his act, put on a suit, and crooned *Satisfaction* with a string quartet, the Rolling Stones wouldn't have changed the music industry. Innovation needs to spark curiosity. It needs to provoke. And curiosity doesn't come from following the rules – it comes from breaking them.

←Cycling Route Network 'Route planner'→#21

#21 Alice is not Alice

I first encountered the real power of curiosity on a rainy afternoon when I wandered into a bookstore and bumped – quite literally – into someone who reminded me of Alice in Wonderland. She took me on a journey, planting ideas like seeds in the fertile soil of my mind, and by the time our conversation was over, I realised she had gotten into my head not through any trickery, but by being genuinely curious. Reflecting on that encounter later, I began to understand how she had done it. It wasn't magic. It was curiosity – an openness to what I was saying that made me feel heard and, in turn, compelled me to share more. The girl gave me a book as a parting gift: *Atlas Shrugged* by Ayn Rand (←#2). It seemed so random at the time. Why give that book? But then again, curiosity is often a bit random.

Now, I know what you're thinking: "This is a lovely story, but it probably never happened. It's one of those writer's inventions, right?" Wrong. The story is real – well, mostly. I was in a bookstore. She was there. And yes, I was unexpectedly gifted that book. But as with all good stories, there are embellishments. The specifics don't really matter. What matters is the encounter itself, the act of curiosity that unfolded that day.

Big bookstores are a treasure trove for people like me. I can lose myself for hours, flipping through books, thinking about all the possibilities they hold, before walking out with a few, eager to explore what lies within. On that day, I didn't know what I was looking for, but I found something. After our little collision, we started talking, and soon, I was telling her everything – about my work as a speaker and a writer, about my endless search for inspiration. I can't remember exactly how we got onto the topic, but I know I handed her a copy of *Hooked* by Nir Eyal, one of my favourites at the time. Later, she emailed me, casually mentioning she didn't think the book was as great as I had made it out to be. "Overhyped," she said. But what struck me most was her disarming honesty. She didn't sugarcoat things, and that made me even more curious about her. No, her name wasn't Alice – but it could have been. Her curiosity was as infectious as Alice's wonder.

←#20 →#22

#22 Curiouser and Curiouser (cried Alice), Too Surprised to Speak Good English

In the days following that encounter, I tried to figure out what had prompted me to share so much with this stranger. Why had I opened up so easily? The answer, of course, was curiosity. Her curiosity drew me in. She asked questions – lots of questions. Each one invited more sharing, more stories, more depth. "What if," she asked. "Why?" "How come?" Every question was like a key, unlocking another part of the conversation. Most of her sentences ended with a question, keeping the dialogue open and expansive. She didn't shut topics down – she built on them, transitioning effortlessly from one subject to the next. Her use of language was simple, but effective. And she used the word interesting so often that I seriously considered making it the title of this book.

Her curiosity wasn't just in her words – it was in her body language. Her wide eyes sparkled with genuine interest. She leaned forward when I spoke, and her hands gestured in a way that made me feel like she was fully engaged. It's the same kind of behaviour you want to see when you present an idea in the business world. If you want people to be curious, you must model curiosity yourself. People mirror what they see, and her curiosity was contagious. The concept of mirroring is well-established in psychology. When we see curiosity in others, we tend to mirror it back. This can be incredibly powerful in both personal and business settings, creating an atmosphere of openness where ideas flow freely. Curious behaviour begets more curious behaviour. And when that happens, innovation thrives.

←#21 #20 →#23

Boldly go where no man has gone before

#23 From Sacrificial Lamb to Success Story

Back in the late 1990s, I was managing a department at a Dutch carpet company that had just been sold to an American corporation. The Americans weren't too keen on our division, which specialised in residential carpet – a small, family-run business sector they weren't interested in. As a result, our division was passed around like a hot potato until it finally landed in my lap. I was young, ambitious, and ready to shake things up. My direct colleagues found me annoying. I kept questioning the status quo, which was a surefire way to become unpopular in a conservative organisation. So, in a move that reeked of desperation, the higher-ups put me forward as a potential leader, likely in the hopes that I'd crash and burn, getting rid of their troublemaker once and for all.

I had four weeks to come up with a plan to save my division – a Hail Mary shot, with a 90% chance of failure. But for me, that 10% was my one chance to prove myself. I stayed up for two straight weeks, crafting a bold, guerrilla-style strategy called *Phoenix from the Ashes*. The idea was to burn down the old ways of doing things and rise again, launching an all-out guerrilla war on our competitors. I was ready. But my boss, a pipe-smoking Frenchman, was not. He insisted I stick to the corporate template for presentations. Reluctantly, I complied, and when I ran the numbers, they showed modest growth – nothing revolutionary, but solid.

Behind the scenes, though, I put my guerrilla tactics into play. We slashed costs for retailers and reinvested the savings into marketing, reaching consumers directly for the first time in 20 years. The team hated it. My sales director even quit in protest. But the results were undeniable – our sales numbers soared, smashing every previous record. The dealers who had initially balked were now cheering.

← #22 #21 #20 → #24

#24 The Gleicher Formula Sparks Curiosity

Then came the presentation – the one I had been dreading. The Americans arrived, led by the feared manager they called The Hawk. He had a reputation for being ruthless, and the nervous energy in the room was palpable. The manager before me walked out shaking his head, white as a ghost. When it was my turn, I launched into the corporate-approved version of my plan. Five slides. Five minutes of soulless drivel. I could see the Americans yawning. Then The Hawk interrupted. "You're that 'young potential', right?" he said, dripping with sarcasm. "What year were you born?"

"Uh, '63," I stammered.
"I'm '65," The Hawk replied, "and no one calls me young anymore. So, is this all you've got?"

At that moment, I made a decision. Ignoring the pleading look from my boss, I pulled up my *Phoenix from the Ashes* presentation. The room went silent. On the screen, I displayed the Gleicher formula – a model I had learned in school and that had stuck with me ever since. It's a simple formula for understanding how change happens: **D x V x F > R.**

- **D**: Dissatisfaction with how things are now.
- **V**: Vision of what is possible.
- **F**: First concrete steps to move toward that vision.
- **R**: Resistance to change.

In short, if dissatisfaction, vision, and action aren't strong enough to overcome resistance, no meaningful change will happen. But if those factors are high enough, the resistance is blown away. I explained the formula, and for the first time that day, The Hawk leaned forward. He was curious

←#23#22#21#20 →#25

#25 Guerrilla Warfare as an Innovative Idea

In my *Phoenix from the Ashes* plan, I didn't just shake the foundations – I levelled the whole house to the ground. Then, I laid out the blueprint for what kind of company we wanted to become. A company with a completely new mindset, different DNA, culture, and management style. A guerrilla strategy was at the heart of it, contrasting sharply with the old, lumbering dinosaur that had been dragging its feet for years. We'd reuse some of the old building blocks, sure, but we'd build smarter ones, more flexible ones, leveraging technology to move faster and adapt quicker.

I presented low, medium, and high growth scenarios, tied to a dynamic budget. The competition's response would determine how fast or slow we'd need to move. The Americans in the room were hooked – you could tell by the way they leaned in. But my European CEO? Not so much. "Are those the numbers?" he barked, checking his watch. This was the first time he'd seen the plan, and I could tell he was losing patience.

"Dynamic budget? What are you, nuts? We need real numbers, not wild dreams. Where's the business case for this fantasy?"

I smiled and said, "I don't have one, because this has never been done before. But I do have one more slide." I clicked to reveal the image of Star Trek's iconic line: *Space, the final frontier... These are the voyages of the starship Enterprise.* The Hawk cracked a smile. He was a Trekkie, and I knew I had him. I explained how we had already quietly taken the first two steps of the plan and what the results were – 30% growth in just one month. "If I'd predicted that," I added, "no one would've believed me."

"Great stuff," The Hawk said. "You'll present this at HQ in Atlanta, but let's tweak the language a bit. Corporate won't love phrases like 'guerrilla warfare' or 'pissing off the competition'."

In the 1990s, I learned an important lesson: an innovative idea doesn't always need a polished business case to sell. But I also learned that breaking conventions comes with a price – it makes you enemies. Later, in 2005, I wanted to grow another company internationally. I used the Gleicher formula (→#24) to get the Board of Directors fired up, which included some well-known politicians and captains of industry. I had them all excited – until I explained how I planned to execute the strategy. Then, the temperature in the room dropped to freezing.

I wasn't interested in the traditional recipe – expensive sales teams, dealers demanding steep margins, and wholesalers who carried no stock. Instead, I proposed using Amazon in the U.S. and Alibaba in China. E-commerce was the future, I argued. But the Board didn't believe me. In 2005, they still thought online sales were a passing fad. That day, I realised my formula doesn't always work. Why? My story didn't spark their curiosity. I hadn't dismantled their preconceived notions.

Still, I quietly moved forward with a small sales team through Amazon and Alibaba. A year later, our growth was spectacular. One board member, who had advised me to ask for forgiveness rather than permission, congratulated me. Another praised me, thinking the success came from traditional methods. When I explained that it was all thanks to e-commerce, chaos ensued. Some board members wanted me fired for ignoring their decision. But the ex-Prime Minister on the Board stood up, glared at the room, and growled, "Stop this nonsense. Well done, young man."

I wasn't fired. Not this time. I got away with it. Like every time.

← #24 #23 #22 #21 #20   → #26

#26 Humans Are Emotional Beings – Be a Storyteller

How do you get people to jump on board with your wild idea? The secret is simple: humans are emotional beings. Rationality often takes a backseat to emotions, even though we like to believe the opposite. Scholars like Piet Vroon and Daniel Kahneman have written extensively about this – our decisions are mostly driven by emotions, with logic playing catch-up. So, if you want your idea to resonate, don't just throw numbers at your audience – tell a story that makes them feel something. People need to see how your idea can change their lives or impact the world around them. And let's not forget: a boardroom is still made up of people. They, too, are driven by curiosity and emotion, even if they try to hide it behind a wall of spreadsheets and jargon. Get them emotionally invested in your idea, and they'll follow you. Their curiosity, something they may be embarrassed to show in such serious settings, can quickly morph into enthusiasm, camouflaged as understanding.

Also, remember: humans are visual creatures. Ditch those dense, text-heavy slides from the boring presentation books. Use images. Paint a picture that sticks in their minds. The most important lesson I've learned is this: people are curious about what they don't know – but it can't feel like an overwhelming plunge into the abyss. That's where you come in. Curiosity is more than just asking questions or encouraging others to ask them. It's the thrill of discovery, the joy of the hunt. It's your job to make that hunt exciting. Make curiosity a shared journey between you and your audience. That way, the idea – no matter how unconventional or out-there it is – becomes something you explore together.

So, what's the first step? Spark their imagination. Whether it's a bold statement, a thought-provoking question, or a challenge they can't resist – make it irresistible. It's like teasing a trailer before the blockbuster drops. You're not giving away the whole story; you're hooking them in, leaving them wanting more. Don't just talk *at* your audience. Challenge them. Make them question what they think they know. Send them on a journey of self-doubt and discovery. A good idea is only a good idea if the story is good. People crave stories. So, don't just present facts and figures; weave them into a narrative that brings your idea to life.

If possible, let your audience touch, feel, or play with your idea – even if it's only in their minds. When people actively engage, they stop being passive listeners and become active participants. Sometimes, the best way to keep them engaged is to leave some things unsaid. A little mystery goes a long way. Let them keep thinking about your idea long after your presentation has ended. The story is more important than sticking to conventional wisdom and forcing your idea into a tidy little business case – believe me. And once you've hooked them, then you can think about the customer, market, finances, and all the serious stuff. But only after you've gotten them curious.

←#25#24#23#22#21#20 →Cycling Route Network 'Measuring Curiosity'

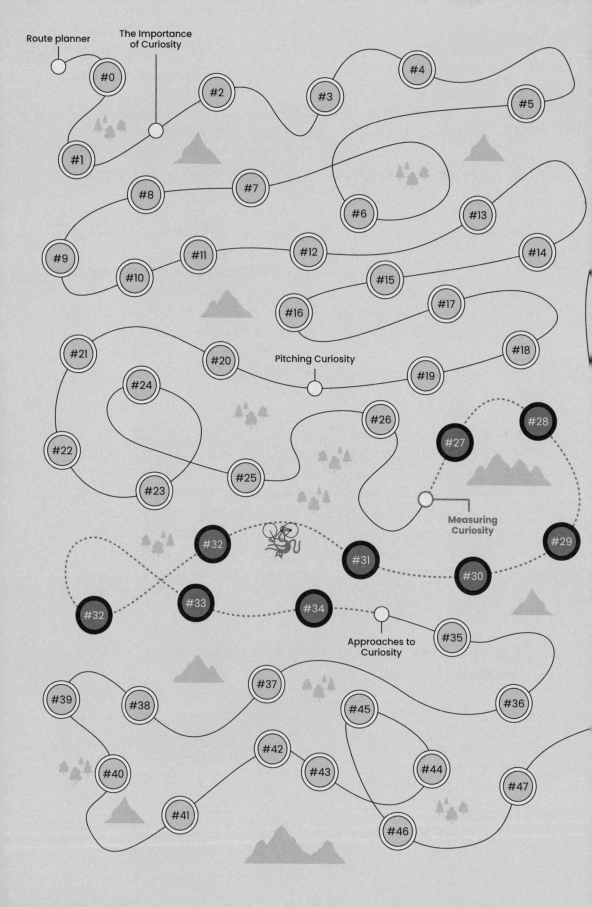

Cycling Route Network 'Measuring Curiosity'

#27 Formula for Change: Logic and Emotion

The Formula for Change, or Gleicher Formula (←#24), is a model that helps gauge how successful a change initiative might be. Originally created by David Gleicher in the 1960s and later refined by Kathie Dannemiller and Steve Cady, the formula provides a framework for understanding the forces at play in organisational change.
The original version looked like this:
C = A x B x D > X

Where:
- **C** = Change
- **A** = Dissatisfaction with the current situation
- **B** = Vision of what's possible
- **D** = First practical steps toward change
- **X** = Costs of the change

But Dannemiller refined it to focus on overcoming resistance to change:
C = D x V x F > R

In this version:
- **D** = Dissatisfaction with how things are now
- **V** = Vision of a better future
- **F** = First concrete steps toward the vision

If the combined product of **D**, **V**, and **F** is greater than resistance (**R**), change is possible. If any one of these factors is low or missing, the effort will likely fail.
Cady's version adds a fourth element:
- **S** = Support to sustain change

So, the final equation looks like this:
D x V x F x S › R

Change is not just a logical process – it's emotional. You have to balance the rational reasons for change with the emotional involvement of the people affected. If you manage to combine both, then resistance will crumble, and you'll create the momentum needed for change.

←#28

#28 Curiosity Killed the Cat, but It Made the Company a Star

"But Rik, curiosity killed the cat." I hear this a lot. Here's what I wrote to a CEO once: Companies too often believe curiosity killed the cat, forgetting that in today's world, it's probably the most valuable tool in their arsenal. Let me make this as simple as possible: curiosity is contagious. One curious person in a company quickly attracts another, and before you know it, you've got a full-blown curiosity epidemic that propels your business forward. In today's hyper-connected world, where a meme in Silicon Valley can go viral in seconds, curiosity spreads faster than wildfire.

Now, imagine a company where curiosity is not just encouraged – it thrives. Everyone – managers, employees, customers – is in on it. The result? A viral curiosity carnival where interest and engagement explode, turning your business into a magnet for attention and innovation. Now imagine the opposite: a company with all the excitement of a brick wall. That company? It's going nowhere fast. Curious companies surf the wave, while the dull, non-curious ones are left floundering, like beached whales in the kiddie pool of irrelevance.

In a world where your neighbour's cat has more TikTok followers than most brands, one thing is clear: curiosity pays. And those companies playing it safe? They're as relevant as a floppy disk at an iPhone launch. Be curious, or get left behind. In the great business casino, the curious hit the jackpot. The rest? They're just watching from the sidelines.

← #27 → #29

We do Everything Differently

#29 Miami Vice and a Pirate

In the early 1990s, I strutted around in Miami Vice-style suits from pricey Italian designers, cruised in hefty German cars, needed a new phone every month, and somehow ended up as the director of a declining A-brand. This brand had long held the misguided belief that thought leadership meant flooding the market with self-proclaimed 'innovations' dreamed up by a pipe-smoking fairy-tale writer who called himself the marketing director. Naturally, we clashed – me with my pirate-like approach, and him with his flowery language and predictable tactics.

Every year, we participated in *the trade show*. You know, the big one where all the brands showed off their latest 'innovations' (and by that, I mean changing a carpet colour and calling it revolutionary). It was also where we were expected to sell, sell, sell. But this time, I had a different idea. Instead of setting up the biggest booth and pushing more so-called innovations down people's throats, I told my team: "We're not selling anything. Nothing. Nada. Zilch." Cue panic. We set up a small, cosy stand – no products, no innovations, just conversations. We were going to listen to our customers. That was the grand idea. The sales team was sceptical. Their entire job, their very identity, was tied to the concept of selling at the trade show. But I didn't care. I made it clear: we were going to listen, not sell. Our theme? Curiosity.

Cue heart attacks. The marketing director nearly choked on his pipe, and the former director – now reporting to me – looked like he was going to pass out. They quickly escalated the situation, and soon I found myself summoned to the European CEO's office. "Have you lost your mind?" he asked. He demanded an explanation and, of course, wanted to know what the Return on Investment (ROI) would be if we didn't sell anything.

I stood my ground. I explained that building relationships and understanding our customers' needs would pay off far more in the long run than immediate sales. He wasn't convinced and, in true temperamental CEO fashion, threatened to fire me. I shrugged it off and suggested he come to the trade show himself. Naturally, he declined. On the day of the trade show, our modest stand was a strange sight among the flashy, product-laden booths of our competitors. At first, our customers were confused – *No products? No sales pitch?* – but soon, we were having meaningful conversations. We asked questions, listened, and gathered valuable insights. We even used questionnaires and multiple-choice forms, which we later processed with a computer to generate actionable data. No one else was doing this.

As you might imagine, my competitors were livid. They weren't selling much either, and suddenly, their massive booths looked ridiculous next to our humble, conversation-driven stand. They sent angry emails to the CEO, who, of course, summoned me once more. He demanded to see the ROI immediately. "I'll show you in six months," I calmly replied. "Let's compare sales then."

And guess what? It worked. Our sales figures soared in the months that followed. Customers appreciated that we had taken the time to understand their needs. Selling is not a means; it's a result. Even the Dutch CEO, who had threatened to fire me multiple times, proudly presented my department's half-year results to the Americans, calling our approach "brilliant". "Curiosity," he said, "is what fuels our success."

I bit my tongue. Little did I know I'd one day write a book about it all – about him, the trade show, and, of course, curiosity.

←#28#27 →#30

#30 The Cinderella Principle: Stop Doing What You've Always Done

Curiosity is the ultimate competitive advantage. Without it, companies get stuck in a "because we've always done it this way" mindset. At some point, every process, every system, every tradition, was invented for a reason. Questioning that reason is curiosity. It's the antidote to stagnation. So, does that reason still exist? Has it changed? Is the solution still relevant? Can we do it differently – not just better – but radically different?

Enter the Formula for Change (←#24#27). There has to be a reason to change. And without curiosity, you won't even see that reason, let alone act on it. In the 1990s, when I took over the declining A-brand (←#29), I quickly realised that more of the same wasn't going to cut it. The entire industry was running on autopilot. Every year, revenues declined, profits dropped, and costs remained stagnant. I told my management team that we needed to do things differently, and over the next six months, we tackled a laundry list of problems.

Here's why we moved fast:
1. We were losing money. Time was of the essence.
2. I preferred short, sharp pain over dragging it out.
3. I was fed up with all the inefficiencies.
4. The competition needed to be stunned into silence.
5. I was ambitious – okay, very ambitious.
6. Each action revealed new opportunities I hadn't seen before.
7. The market was wide open, and I wanted to grab it now.

Let me give you two examples – nothing earth-shattering, but it all started with curiosity.

Example: The Ugly Hangers.
Our sample materials were hideous. Heavy, clunky hangers with carpet swatches – the same ones every brand used, made by the same supplier. The only difference was the brand's logo slapped onto the same dull grey plastic. These things had existed for decades, and no one had ever questioned them. Together with my marketer (not the pipe-smoking guy), we spent days figuring out how these samples were used, what worked, what didn't, and why. Then we teamed up with a Dutch designer to create something functional but also beautiful – something that would rewrite the rules of sample materials.

The first prototypes were promising. We refined them through trial and error, like a scrappy startup, and started testing them with dealers. The result? Big fun. But there was one problem: cost. These new samples were expensive to produce. We couldn't afford to replace all our dealers' sample materials in one go. That led to the inevitable cheese slicer discussions. Can we make it cheaper? Do we need all the bells and whistles? Does it really need to be a Big Bang rollout? At times like these, I get stubborn. I had a vision, and I wasn't letting go.

←#29#28#27 →#31

#31 Evidence

Our new sample materials were stunning, but the cost was still too high. Feeling frustrated, I did something I rarely do – I talked to my wife about it. I showed her the samples, and after testing them, she asked the simplest, most brilliant question: "Why do the dealers get these for free?"

I was speechless. Was I so stuck in the industry's patterns that I hadn't questioned this? The idea that sample materials couldn't be sold? That night, I tossed and turned, thinking about it. In our industry, samples were free, but in other sectors, like wallpaper, dealers paid for them. Why not us? This one question led me to reorganise our entire dealer network, something no one had thought of in 30 years.

I started charging for sample materials, and the first dealers quickly claimed their territories. Soon after, the ball started rolling, and I made another bold move: I fired most of our sales reps and replaced them with merchandisers. The sales reps had been stuck in the old routine – driving from dealer to dealer, talking football and politics, and barely moving the needle. The merchandisers, on the other hand, could actually deliver on my promises to the dealers. The result? We sold the sample materials, reinvested that money into marketing, and the dealers, having made an investment, were now much more loyal. Our competitors, still giving away free samples, didn't know what hit them.

Revenue soared, and we slashed our costs. All thanks to one question from my wife.

Curiosity as a competitive advantage. It's not just about coming up with ideas. It's about seeing the patterns you're stuck in and daring to question them. I often see speakers saying you should swim with the current, that it's easier. Sure, it's easier – but easier isn't the goal. Swimming with the current is what everyone does. Swimming against it – that's what makes you unique. That's what we did. And it worked.

←#30#29#28#27 →#32

Dreamer or doer

#32 My Revenge on the 'Hard Workers'

In the business world, we have two types of companies: 'noun companies' and 'verb companies'. Noun companies are the classic 'hard workers'. They focus on concrete goals, efficiency, and measurable results. They're goal-oriented, functional, and efficient. On the other hand, verb companies are the 'dreamers' (→#43). They thrive on curiosity, exploration, and innovation. And while they may be seen as 'playing around', especially by the noun companies, it's this playful approach that proves to be far more effective in times of rapid change.

The problem with noun companies is that they're static. They're glued to their established categories and definitions, afraid to deviate from their set paths. Meanwhile, verb companies are dynamic. They're constantly evolving, open to new ideas, and unafraid to ask questions and think outside the box. Curiosity is their fuel, and it allows them to innovate and adapt when change inevitably comes knocking.

Here's the irony: the companies who think they're working the hardest are often the ones struggling the most. They're grinding away in their well-defined categories while the verb companies, the 'dreamers', are the ones that thrive. They're the ones who see the future, create new paths, and aren't afraid to ask questions or explore uncharted territory.

So, for all the dreamers out there, hidden within your organisations: keep dreaming. Keep exploring. Keep asking questions. In the end, it's the dreamers who become the doers, the ones who change the world.

←#31#30#29#28#27 →#33

#33 Simultaneously, Two Sides of the Same Coin

After one of my workshops, a tech company CEO called me provocative. I think she meant it as a compliment. We had been discussing the whole 'dreamers vs. doers' thing, and I told her they weren't opposites at all. Dreamers and doers have to work together. This is where Todd Kashdan's research comes into play. He's done extensive work on curiosity, well-being, and psychological flexibility. Kashdan talks about two types of curiosity: exploratory and executive. Exploratory curiosity is about asking questions, imagining new possibilities, and stepping outside the norm. It's the dreamer's playground. Executive curiosity, on the other hand, is about action – getting things done. It's what the doers use to turn ideas into reality.

These two types of curiosity actually reinforce each other. Together, they create a powerful dynamic where innovation and execution coexist and thrive. Instead of marginalising dreamers after the brainstorming phase, companies should keep them around to see the process through. This synergy between dreamers and doers is essential for success, especially in our rapidly changing world. Think of it like building a cathedral. You need both the visionaries (dreamers) and the craftspeople (doers) to get it done. They need to collaborate throughout the entire process, not just in the beginning or at the end. It's a dance, an ongoing dialogue where ideas and execution continuously fuel each other.

←#32#31#30#29#28#27 →#34

#34 Idiot

So how did I foster collaboration between dreamers and doers in my own organisation? A few things come to mind:
1. Create a culture of respect: Make sure both groups know their contributions are valued. Dreamers aren't just pie-in-the-sky thinkers, and doers aren't just mindless executors. Both are essential.
2. Facilitate communication: Set up regular meetings or workshops where dreamers and doers can exchange ideas and collaborate on projects.
3. Offer joint training: Teach skills that help these two groups understand each other better.
4. Encourage cross-functional teams: Let dreamers and doers work together on the same projects.
5. Value both the process and the outcome: Don't just celebrate the finished product. Appreciate the journey of exploration and experimentation.

One evening, during a dinner with the CEO who had called me provocative (←#32), I told her I used to sign all my internal emails with TIIC – The Idiot In Charge. She burst out laughing, loudly declaring to the entire restaurant, "This man is an idiot!" It was one of those moments where I felt my face turning bright red, but deep down, I kind of liked it.

←#33#32#31#30#29#28#27 →Cycling Route Network 'Approaches to Curiosity'

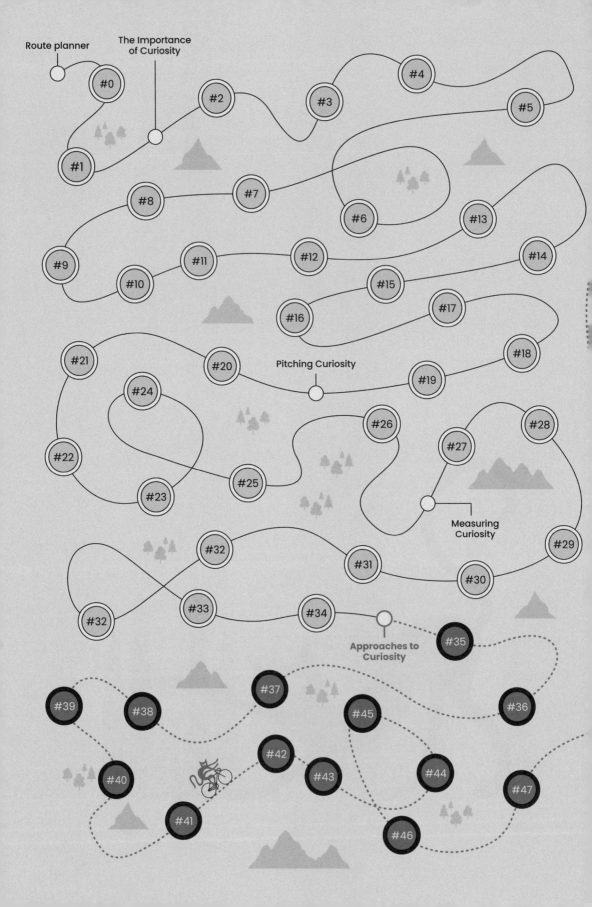

Cycling Route Network 'Approaches to Curiosity'

#35 Engaged Employees

Curiosity isn't just for innovation. It's a huge factor in employee engagement too. When people are curious, they're more interested in their work. They come up with creative solutions and get excited about challenges. And here's the funny part: I stumbled upon this realisation by accident. As a manager, I used curiosity without even knowing I was doing it (←#24#25).

See, I don't think linearly. My plans often seem like they're full of holes, leaving space for people to fill in the gaps themselves. At first, this frustrates some people. But then something magical happens: I pique their curiosity, and suddenly they're motivated to figure out what they're missing. I once received feedback from a manager at a large German company. After a two-day session at London Business School, she said she had spent the first day wondering how all my exercises fit together. But that curiosity kept her engaged, and by the second day, she started seeing the bigger picture. "I discovered it myself," she said, "and that's what made it so powerful."

When employees can discover things on their own, it leads to a deeper emotional connection with their work and the organisation. Curiosity sparks engagement, and that engagement drives performance.

←#36

#36 The Art of Listening

Back at that small, cosy stand at the trade show (←#29), we didn't just listen to our customers – we really listened. And that listening led to new ideas that skyrocketed our revenue in the months that followed. Companies love to talk about the importance of listening to customers and employees. But here's the thing: most of them are terrible at it. They run surveys with suggestive questions, use leading language, and design questionnaires that practically force a positive response. The worst part? They pat themselves on the back afterward, thinking they've done a great job of gathering feedback.

Listening is an art, and it requires more than just asking the right questions. It requires genuine curiosity – being open to hearing what you don't want to hear as much as what you do. When I first instructed my team to listen before that particular trade show (←#29), I had to train them in the art of listening. It wasn't as easy as it sounded. But the results were worth it. Later, when I developed the Net Curiosity Score (NCS) as a KPI, that insight proved invaluable. In one of my earliest sales meetings, I laid out the importance of finding out how we could make our customers' lives easier, better, and more enjoyable. But the only way to do that was through genuine listening – not just hearing what we wanted to hear. We needed to really understand how we were perceived in the market and where we could improve.

←#35 →#37

#37 Framing and Nudging

People's minds are surprisingly easy to steer – yes, you can nudge their thoughts, their perceptions, their decisions. Enter framing, the magic trick where you present information just so, and boom – people start processing it differently. And then there's nudging, where you give them a gentle, almost imperceptible push (think: *"Oh, go on then"*) to guide their choices. The beauty? You're not stealing their freedom – just… steering them a bit. It's subtle, maybe a little sneaky, but come on, it's not evil. It's everywhere – marketing, politics, media – you name it. If you haven't noticed, it's because it's working on you.

Now, let's bring this mind-magic into the business world. In meetings, leaders can use framing and nudging to influence the room. Want people to really think? Use framing to shape the conversation. Want them to think outside the box? Give them a little nudge to stop staring at last quarter's sales chart and start thinking about what comes next. Curiosity cranks up, and suddenly the energy in the room shifts. That spreadsheet? Forgotten.

Case in point: My eldest daughter's college thesis. She asked me to read it, and – bam – I was hooked. Her experiments showed that if you start by throwing people into big, abstract ideas (you know, like galaxies or philosophical rabbit holes), good luck bringing them back to earth to think about practical stuff. On the flip side, get people stuck in the here and now – hello, to-do lists – and it's a Herculean task to get them thinking about anything more creative than 'what's for lunch'.

So, apply this to your next meeting. Start with operational talk – last month's numbers, that project status – and watch curiosity die a slow, quiet death. People switch to optimise mode – tweaking what already exists, no room for new ideas. But flip it around: Start with some exploration – a wide-open, "what if?" vibe – and curiosity kicks in like a shot of espresso. Dynamic, flexible thinking takes over, and suddenly, that boring meeting just became a whole lot more interesting. Maybe even fun. (Shocking, I know.) The secret to a killer meeting? Structure your agenda strategically. Lead with curiosity, and trust me – you'll get results. Most management meetings? They miss this boat entirely.

←#36#35 →#38

#38 Antidote and Competitive Advantage

Curiosity. The ultimate antidote to hearing what you want to hear. I said this in a keynote in the '90s, and – spoiler alert – it's still true. Real curiosity? It doesn't come with blinders on. It's all wide-eyed, hungry for the truth, no matter how messy that truth might be. You want real feedback on your product? None of those leading, 'nudge-nudge' questions (←#37) that sneakily push people to the answers you want. No. Try this: "What's your most memorable experience with our product or service?" Bam. Open-ended, no boundaries. You'll get the raw, unfiltered, sometimes awkward, sometimes glowing truth. But that's what curiosity is about: truth, not just the answer you hoped for.

Curiosity gives you a serious competitive edge. It's not just about gathering data; it's about seeing what others don't. At sixteen, I learned programming (yes, back when coding was a wild frontier). I quickly realised computers make connections that humans can't, because we're too busy letting our emotions get in the way. In the early '90s – pre-internet, mind you – I had a sales program built. It was a *primitive CRM*, tracking more than just sales. Data was – and still is – king, but the quality of that data depends on how you collect it. That's where curiosity steps in. It's not just a tool. It's a philosophy. A mindset. It cracks open doors to insights you didn't even know were hiding. And you know where that leads? Growth. Real, sustainable, competitive growth.

Curious companies? They don't just keep up – they lead. They spot the opportunities and trends *before* everyone else, which gives them a sustainable edge. Look at Apple and the iPhone. Sure, they weren't the first to make a smartphone, but they were the first to make the smartphone. You know, the one that turned the whole industry upside down. Apple didn't just ask, "What do people need?" They asked, "What do they really want?" And then they built it before people even knew they wanted it. User-friendly, sleek design, crazy good functionality. Boom. Market dominance.

But hold on – let's not pretend it was all Apple. It was the Apple of Steve Jobs. That guy was driven by curiosity. I was a huge fan. Sadly, though, I fear that Apple today might be inching toward what I call the Chernobyl Syndrome (←#6). That's when companies get too comfortable, stop questioning, stop asking, "What if?" They start believing they know everything. And when that happens? Curiosity dies. And without curiosity, so does innovation.

←#37#36#35 →#39

#39 Outsiders and Insiders

Outsiders often spot things that – bizarrely enough – insiders just can't see (←#31). Why? Well, let's break it down:
- Fresh Eyes: Outsiders come in with zero baggage. No biases, no "this is how we've always done it" nonsense. They get to look at the situation like it's a puzzle waiting to be solved. Insiders? More like *"this puzzle is missing pieces, so let's not even try"*.
- Too Close for Comfort: Insiders are way too cosy with the day-to-day grind. You know what happens when you're too close? Tunnel vision. You stop seeing the bigger picture and start obsessing over the Post-It notes.
- Corporate Blind Spots: Company cultures are like comfy blankets that smother any fresh ideas. Outsiders? No such blanket. They aren't bound by the corporate groupthink. They stroll in with innovative solutions while insiders are busy defending the status quo.
- No Fear, No Filter: Insiders are often scared stiff of stepping on toes – "better not suggest this, or I might be wearing a box instead of a desk next week" – but outsiders? They'll tell it like it is, no sweat.
- Mixing Things Up: Outsiders bring a wild mix of experiences. They've seen things, done things, weird things in other sectors, and guess what? That's where magic happens.

Curiosity turns insiders into outsiders. Curious people step back, see the big picture, and actually notice stuff. They stop being stuck in their tiny bubbles and start asking, "What if?" It's like putting on glasses that finally let you see what's been right in front of you. Curiosity blasts through those corporate blinders and gives you the guts to ask tough questions – like, why are we doing this ridiculous thing in the first place?

It sets the stage for unfiltered dialogue and, dare I say it, innovative breakthroughs. It's the ultimate cross-sector power-up.

Let's be real: most companies are too scared to experiment because of the R-word. Risk. But guess what? Companies with a high NCS (←#49) don't see risk as the enemy. They see it as part of the ride. And yeah, they win more because they're willing to fall flat on their faces every now and then.

←#38 #37 #36 #35 →#40

#40 The Space Pirate in *The Martian*, ten lessons learned

I've always been a bit of a dreamer – not the "stare out the window and imagine unicorns" kind, but the "what if we tried something insane and saw what happens" kind. Luckily for me, I always had doers by my side – people who'd roll their eyes at my wild ideas and say, "Okay, fine, let's try it." Those experiments? They led to even more wild ideas.

Quick tip: Innovation isn't a one-and-done. It's more like up-innovation, cross-innovation, deep-innovation. Once you catch that curiosity bug, it spreads. Fast. People love talking about the successes (because it makes us sound smart), but trust me – there were plenty of oh-no-what-have-we-done moments too. Days where the light at the end of the tunnel was nothing but a flicker, and we seriously questioned our sanity. But here's the deal: We developed some tricks to deal with all those soul-crushing disappointments:
- Let it out: Yeah, we felt crappy. But we didn't shove it down. We said it. Out loud. "This sucks." Because bottling it up just leads to a mental meltdown.
- Analyse it: What happened? What did we screw up? And most importantly, what can we learn from this glorious failure?
- Pivot like a pro: Stubbornness is a virtue in the innovation world.

Adjust, adapt, find another path.
- Support system: When things went south, we vented to our crew. And sometimes, a random outsider, because fresh perspectives can save your bacon.
- Keep moving: Even if it's baby steps. Progress is progress – and no step forward is too small to celebrate.
- Small victories are everything: A win is a win, even if it's microscopic. Celebrate like you just landed on Mars.
- Stay positive: This wasn't just 'rah-rah' motivation. We literally trained ourselves to see opportunities instead of obstacles.

Which brings me to Mark Watney, aka The Space Pirate in *The Martian*. That guy nailed the innovation mindset. Stranded on Mars with no hope of rescue? He didn't curl up and cry. He improvised and became a one-man innovation machine. Honestly, if you want a crash course in creativity and grit, *The Martian* is your jam.

In my workshops, I make participants watch it and jot down lessons on innovation. Here are the top 10 Watney takeaways:

1. Uncertainty is a given: Just because you succeeded today doesn't mean tomorrow isn't going to punch you in the face. Watney's stuck on Mars because of bad luck, not failure. Kodak, Nokia, auto giants – sometimes, it's just a crapshoot.
2. Persevere: Keep busy or you'll drown in despair. Action beats fear, every time.
3. Endurance matters more than speed: Everyone loves a sprint these days, but long-distance innovation is where it's at.
4. Setbacks happen: Watney's farm blows up. Yeah, it sucks. But you adapt or die – literally.
5. One problem at a time: When everything feels impossible, break it down into bite-sized chunks. Solve this, then solve that. Repeat.
6. Blind optimism? Hell yeah: Watney *decides* he's going to survive, and that's half the battle. You need that level of crazy confidence to push through.
7. Ingenuity wins: He's on Mars with nothing, and still, he figures out how to grow potatoes. The lesson? Use what you've got – it's prob-

ably more than you think.
8. Trust your gut: NASA's advice? Meh. Watney follows his instincts, and it pays off. Sometimes, your gut is smarter than the experts.
9. Celebrate the little wins: Watney colonises Mars? Huge! Declares himself a "space pirate"? *Legendary*. Every step counts.
10. Human connection matters: The first human voice Watney hears after his isolation? Priceless. At the end of the day, it's the people who keep us going.

The D in the Formula for Change (←#27)? Watney lives it. He makes a gutsy, all-or-nothing move with no guarantees. Why? Because not trying means certain doom. That's CRC – Compelling Reason to Change, the moment where you say, "We either go big or go home." Watney? He goes BIG.

←#39#38#37#36#35 →#41

#41 All-In and the Tourist Principle

It takes guts to leave the comfy harbour and dive headfirst into the unknown. Let's face it – most of us only do it when we're cornered, when standing still is no longer an option. We don't go all-in unless we're forced to, right? We associate this kind of crazy, high-stakes move with people like Elon Musk. Half the world thinks he's a genius, the other half thinks he's a lunatic with a Twitter habit (sorry, X habit). He makes people nervous. Even I sometimes wonder if the line between crazy and brilliant is *wafer-thin* when I see his posts. But hey, you don't have to be Elon Musk to show a little more guts. Maybe we don't need to wait until we're in full Watney-on-Mars mode (←#40) to make a bold move. How do we tackle innovation before it becomes a crisis-level tsunami that makes us run for the hills? A few ideas:

- Accept risks: Don't wait until the path is 100% safe. By then, it's too easy, too boring, and definitely not distinctive. Risk is part of the game.
- Build a squad: Surround yourself with people who've got your back. Even CEOs need a crew. The ones who try to do it all solo? Yeah, they're the ones freaking out at 2 a.m.
- Support network = two-way street: Ask for help when you need it, but be the kind of person who gives support when someone else needs a boost. Reciprocity, baby.
- Expect setbacks: Watney hit plenty of bumps on Mars (literal craters), and you will too. Plan all you want, but know that shit happens – deal with it and learn from it.
- Keep learning: Curiosity is the secret sauce that makes every setback an opportunity to level up. The more you learn, the less freaked out you'll be when things go sideways.
- Persevere: Eyes on the prize. Remember why you started in the first place.
- Celebrate everything: Even the tiniest win deserves a mini-party. These victories fuel you for the long haul.

Now, let me tell you about my trip to Budapest. I was invited to speak to a group of bank CEOs. The woman who had seen me at London Business School picked me up from the hotel, and on the drive, she told me something that stuck. When she first started at the bank, they let her be a 'tourist' in the company for a few weeks. Yep, a tourist. What a brilliant idea! Because how often do CEOs just wander around their own companies without an agenda? When do they not show up to solve problems or give orders? It's rare.

But when leaders take a step back and act like tourists in their own companies – when they just observe – magic happens. They spot things no one else does, things the locals (the employees) overlook because they're too close to the action. In the daily grind of optimising processes and keeping the wheels turning, exploration gets tossed aside. The tourist principle? It flips that script. Leaders get to walk around like outsiders, and suddenly, hidden gems start popping up everywhere. So, here's my challenge: Be a tourist in your own company. Take a stroll. Ask questions. Notice what's going on without trying to fix anything right away. You might find a lot more than you expected.

←#40#39#38#37#36#35 →#42

Geography of Thought

#42 Eastern vs. Western Thinking

Ever wonder why Easterners and Westerners don't think the same way? Richard E. Nisbett did, and he wrote a killer book about it: The *Geography of Thought*. According to Nisbett, these differences go way back – like ancient Greece vs. China back. It all stems from ecological, social, and philosophical roots, plus centuries of education systems. Eastern thought is holistic – they see the whole field, not just the star player. It's all about relationships, processes, and the big picture. Western thought? More goal-oriented, focused on the individual, with a love affair with categories and formal logic. We love sticking things in boxes and connecting the dots with straight lines. Nisbett drops a cool metaphor about Eastern thinking: it's like having eyes in the back of your head. Curiosity at its best – not obsessed with a goal, just keeping an eye on the unexpected. It's like looking at the world through a wider lens, seeing what others miss. Western thinking, on the other hand? Eyes on the ball. All about the goal. No distractions allowed.

It's the same vibe I get from my beach chair model: The Westerners are focused on the beach chairs (i.e., optimisation). They refuse to get up and look around. The Easterners? They're getting up, stretching their legs, and maybe even heading down to the water to surf the waves of exploration. Western companies stick to their KPIs and balanced scorecards, eyes glued to the sand. Eastern companies? They're checking out the big picture and maybe spotting that grey rhino that's been charging toward them for a while. (Yeah, that thing we all see coming but ignore until it's too late.)

And here's the irony. The unexpected isn't usually some crazy black swan out of left field. It's usually the grey rhino – massive, obvious, and heading right for us. We see it, but we keep our eyes on the ball and hope it'll magically turn away. That's what Nisbett calls linear thinking – classic Western style. We love our logical progressions and causal chains. The East? They think in circles. It's all about process, context, and how everything's connected. Westerners break things down into pieces, aiming for concrete goals. Easterners focus on the journey, knowing that everything's in flux. Maybe there's a lesson in that for all of us.

←#41#40#39#38#37#36#35 →#43

#43 Nouns and Verbs: Go with Alice

In his book (←#42), Nisbett asks the killer question: Is the world of organisations made up of nouns or verbs? (←#32) Well, if you ask Westerners, the answer's obvious – it's nouns, baby! Categories. Rules. We're talking stuff in neat little boxes. But ask Easterners, and they're all about verbs – relationships, connections, constant movement. Western thinking is all about nouns. Classify, categorise, slap a label on it. It's like an episode of *Tidying Up* with Marie Kondo. Everything gets put in a drawer, separate from the context it lives in. Want to make a decision? Easy – just follow the rules, policies, the stuff that's already laid out. Simple, right? But, also… boring.

Eastern thinking? They're over here with their verbs. It's not about isolating things – it's about the interactions, how one thing influences another. Decisions? They're more like jazz – improvised, context-driven. One thing changes, and *whoosh* – the whole dynamic shifts. So, which mindset wins in today's chaotic, fast-moving world? Curious companies – the ones that go full-on verb mode. They're nimble, they're constantly asking, "What's next?" and they embrace the unknown. They don't sit around waiting for a rulebook to tell them what to do. No, they're out there creating new rules as they go. These companies are like Alice in Wonderland – open-minded, moving forward without needing a fixed goal, and letting the journey shape the destination. It's a Wonderland thing: any road will get you there if you don't know where you're going, because the journey itself is the point.

On the flip side, noun companies? They cling to the familiar. They're all about exploitation, squeezing every last drop out of what they already know, refining what's safe. But they've got a serious blind spot: they're stuck in the past. The context around them changes, but they're too rigid to adapt. While verb companies are out there exploring, noun companies are stuck in the same tired loop, missing opportunities right under their noses. The real world? It's more verb than noun. It's messy, it's constantly shifting, and it doesn't care about your neat little categories. Curious companies that roll with the chaos, that are always re-evaluating and rethinking the game, are the ones that win. They're Alice, wandering Wonderland, seeing the world in motion, and recognising that success doesn't come from sticking to the same old script – it comes from embracing the unknown.

In my primary school days, we learned about action words and thing words – and this is exactly the same deal. There are action companies – those that create and evolve – and thing companies – those that milk what's already there until the well runs dry. You need both, sure, but only one is really built for the future. Companies today have a choice: Do they cling to the old way and risk being left behind, or do they embrace the chaos, like Alice, and jump into the unknown? The future belongs to the companies that choose to explore, to question, and to adapt. The rest? Well, they'll be stuck in their static noun world until they slowly fade into irrelevance. The choice is yours: be a noun or be a verb.

> *If you don't know where you are going, any way is the right way.*

← #42 #41 #40 #39 #38 #37 #36 #35   → #44

The Cinderella Principle: Don't Look at Things as They Are

#44 Cinderella

During Covid-19, I had a cosy bubble with my daughter and two of my grandkids. Disney movies? Oh, we watched a bunch. But *Bambi*? Hell no. I'm still traumatised from seeing that as a six-year-old. So, we landed on *Cinderella*. Dutch version? Nowhere to be found. So I became the voice-over narrator. Perks of doing it yourself? You get to choose where to soften the blow and where to shine the spotlight.

So, there's Cinderella – rags, chores, dreams of the ball. Meanwhile, the wicked stepmom and her fashion-disaster daughters are living it up, dressed to the nines. Cinderella? Not so much. But, of course, in swoops the Fairy Godmother. Pumpkin on the ground. Rats scurrying around. Cinderella, ever the practical one, takes a look and goes, "Yeah, this is not happening." The Fairy Godmother just smiles, waves her wand, and drops the golden line:

> *Don't look at things as they are but look at things as they can become.*

BAM! The pumpkin? A coach. The rats? Footmen. Mice? Now majestic white horses. That's the Cinderella Principle, folks. And ever since I heard that line, it's been in every keynote, every workshop: Don't see things as they are – see them as they can become. Now, think about companies. Noun companies see things exactly as they are. Fixed. Static. Zero creativity. Zero curiosity. Verb companies? They see potential. They're dynamic. They don't look at a pumpkin and see a vegetable – they see a carriage. Verb companies are all about action, context, and growth. They understand the world isn't static, and new things can grow from chaos. The catch? Dare to be like Cinderella. Dare to dream up new possibilities, to deconstruct the ordinary, and build something new. Trust me, you'll meet resistance. People will call it 'nonsense', 'daydreaming', or some fancy term like 'reframing'. But they'll fight it. I see it all the time: companies throw together an innovation department – bean bags, ping pong tables, whiteboards, graffiti on the walls. Looks like Wonderland. But is it? Are they playing 'as if' tea party? Or is there some buzzkill who barges in demanding to see the business case, the ROI? And with that, the magic dies, and so does Wonderland. Poof.

←#43#42#41#40#39#38#37#36#35 →#45

#45 Cinderella and Time

Let's rewind to February 2, 2017. I made three predictions about the future. The reactions? A mixed bag. From, "Well, that sounds good in theory, but it's never gonna happen," to "Man, what kind of nonsense are you spouting?" But also a few dreamers with, "Yes, I want that too!" Here's the thing: Will these predictions ever happen exactly as I imagined? No clue. If they'll happen? Oh, I'm pretty sure. When they'll happen? No idea. So what's the point, right? Let me tell you.

> **Prediction 1: Time Will Become the New Currency**
> Time is the ultimate asset – if you can call it that. We spend time making money, only to turn around and use that money to buy ourselves more time. Ridiculous, isn't it? Time is finite. You can't buy it, you can't hold onto it – you can only lose it or make it valuable. I'm convinced time is about to become the only real currency. It always was, but we're finally at the tipping point where it's obvious. I love that line from *Fight Club*:

> *We buy things we don't need with money we don't have to impress people we don't like.*

That's about to change. People care less about money and a whole lot more about quality of life. They want experiences. Take public transport. It's still measured by cost – getting you from A to B. But really, its true value is time. It should be about creating a great experience during the journey, making sure people are investing their time wisely. Same with self-driving cars (aka the new kind of automobiles). It's not the car itself that's valuable – it's the time it frees up for you. If public transport doesn't figure this out, self-driving cars will steal their lunch money. Both are selling the same thing: quality time. Time you can use to do anything but focus on driving.

Quick story. I was in a café in Ghent where the owner was annoyed that people were hogging his Wi-Fi, buying one coffee, and staying for hours. I told him, "Dude, flip your business model." Stop selling coffee. Start selling time. Charge people for how long they hang out, and all drinks are included. I'm convinced this shift will happen in every industry. Those who figure it out first? They'll reap the rewards.

Prediction 2: The Sharing Economy Will Create an App for Everything, Really Everything

The sharing economy isn't new, but it's picking up steam. We've realised we don't need to own stuff – we just need access to it. Saves us time and money. Why spend hours earning cash to buy expensive things when you can rent them for a fraction of the cost?

Enter apps. There's going to be an app for literally everything. That's what technology does – makes life easier, gives us back more time. And as ownership becomes less important, so will the need for money. Why? Because if you're not buying things but just borrowing them, you don't need that much cash. I see this evolving into a world where we're not even exchanging money anymore. We'll be trading time for time. The platforms of the future? They won't be helping you share stuff. They'll be helping you share time. And the more time you share, the more time you have for yourself.

Prediction 3: New Types of Communities Will Cause a Shift in Power

The internet is breaking down old power structures. We're moving away from top-down governments and heading toward bottom-up communities. People are taking control, and this isn't a pipe dream – it's already happening. Think hippies but with better tech. Creativity is exploding in places like San Francisco (no coincidence there), the birthplace of divergent thinking. The internet is driving a massive power shift, and the old guard is terrified. They see their control slipping, so they're clamping down. But here's the thing: The New World has already won. It's all about transparency, distributed authority, and people-powered movements. The old world can't survive in this new era, no matter how hard they fight.

Those were my three predictions in 2017. Some of it's already happening. The rest? It's coming. My advice: Don't fight it. Step into it. Be curious. Be open. Taste it. Feel it. Learn how it works and how society's changing. Then go back to your business, tear it apart, rebuild it to fit the future, and scale up – fast. Because time, my friends, is running out.

← #44 #43 #42 #41 #40 #39 #38 #37 #36 #35 → #46

#46 Aha Moment

So, what's the point of the Cinderella Principle (←#45)? Why bother seeing things as they can become, not just as they are? Especially when you know those things may never happen or at least not in the way you imagined. The Cinderella Principle isn't about predicting the future. It's about thinking beyond today's limitations and giving yourself and your company the chance to imagine something totally new. It's about opening up your mind to possibilities, sparking new business models, and giving you an edge over the competition. Companies that think this way don't wait around for change to slap them in the face – they're proactive, they take risks, and they explore the unknown. Thinking about the future, like time becoming currency and customer experience (←#45), isn't about getting it right – it's about forcing yourself to rethink your current services. When you're constantly asking questions about what could be, you naturally prepare yourself for whatever crazy change actually comes your way. It's not about predicting the exact future; it's about preparing your mind for rapid, unpredictable change. You're not caught flat-footed. When things go sideways, you're already in the habit of thinking flexibly, ready to pounce on new opportunities.

Back when I was "just" a manager (yes, that was a lifetime ago), I used to sneak in a future idea or a wild concept into my management team meetings every other week – no matter how absurd it seemed. Guess what? It worked like a creativity booster shot. It broke through the resistance to change, loosened up our thinking, and gave us a fresh lens for the rest of the meeting. Little did I know, I was framing our thinking (←#37), giving us permission to dream big. And then, later, while watching Cinderella with my grandkids, I had my own aha moment.

> *Don't look at things as they are, but look at things as they can become.*

That line wasn't just for Cinderella – it's for every business looking to escape its own pumpkin.

←#45#44#43#42#41#40#39#38#37#36#35 →#47

#47 The proof of the pudding

Let's get real. My 2017 predictions (←#45) might seem like they didn't pan out. But here's the thing: the point isn't about being right. The point is about predicting in the first place, so you get your mind ready for when things do change. I know what you're thinking: *"Nice excuse, Rik. But this is business. If your predictions don't hold up, we're not interested."* Fair enough, I've spent enough time in your world to get it. You want proof. I feel you. But take a second before you write me off like some corporate Tintin wandering through Businessland with nothing but wide-eyed wonder.

Let's break it down:
- Growth of the Sharing Economy: Airbnb. Uber. These platforms flipped travel and accommodation upside down. Sure, in Belgium it's still subtle, but pop over to Amsterdam, and you'll see Airbnb's everywhere. And those shared scooters and bikes? They're creeping into big cities and small towns alike.
- Rise of Digital Currencies: Love it or hate it, cryptocurrency is real, and it's changing the financial game. Hell, even my banking app pays me in coins for sharing my data. Coincidence? Nope.
- Bottom-up Communities: The internet is home to all sorts of bottom-up movements that challenge the top-down systems. From positive change to the wild world of conspiracy theories, it's clear central authority is crumbling. Houston, we have a problem. Wait… there's no Houston anymore. Oops, we are the problem…
- Transparency and Decentralisation: Blockchain is opening up new frontiers in transparency, especially in finance and logistics. And yes, there are business cases. Yes, real ones.

- Experience Over Ownership: The younger generations? They want experiences, not stuff. The whole notion of owning things is so last century.
- Shifts in Work: Freelancing, remote working, flexible hours – they're the new normal. The old work-to-buy-more cycle is starting to crack, and people are realising they can work differently and live better.

So, yeah, my predictions? They're not just hypothetical musings. They're happening. Slowly, sure, but we're witnessing the early stages of a major transformation in how we live, work, and think. I wrote about this in *The Guide to The Ecosystem Economy* and back in *Managers The Day After Tomorrow*.

←#46#45#44#43#42#41#40#39#38#37#36#35
→Cycling Route Network 'Paradox'

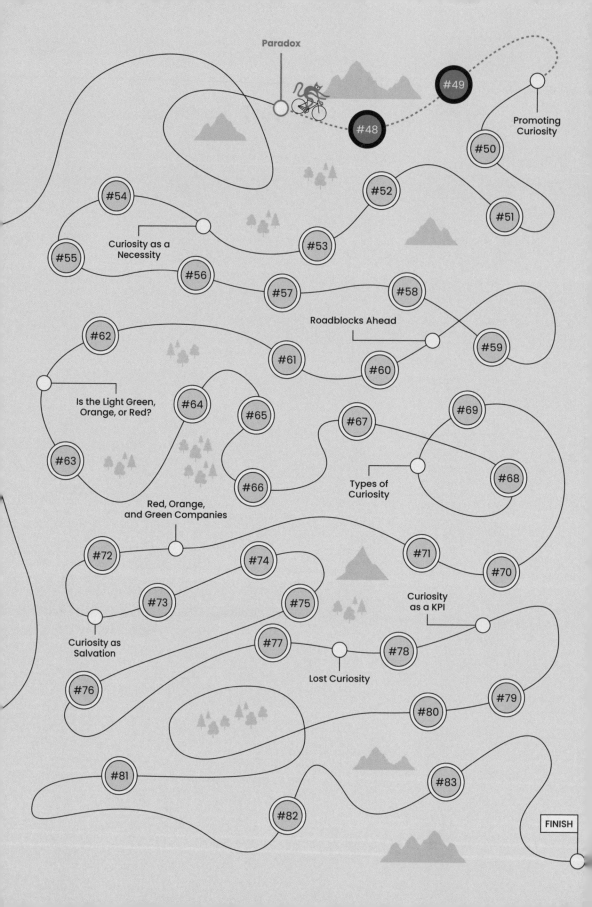

Cycling Route Network 'Paradox'

#48 Front-Runners and Rear-Guarders

> *Any sufficiently advanced technology is indistinguishable from magic. – Arthur C. Clarke*

Clarke nailed it. Think about blockchain, AI, the sharing economy – it all feels like magic until you realise it's reality. New technologies and economic models are shaking the very foundation of traditional structures. So, about those 2017 predictions (←#45)... You think they didn't come true? Really? (←#47) Maybe we're just not looking closely enough. Those little waves? They're getting bigger, my friends. Surfers can spot the good ones on the horizon, but if you're standing on the shore? You might miss the brewing storm.

Can't you feel the tipping point? Or maybe it's already happened, and you didn't even notice. The resistance to change, the rise of rear-guard actions – you see it everywhere. Politicians peddling nostalgia for the "good old days". Dystopian futures splashed across our screens. It's the old guard clinging to what's familiar while front-runners charge ahead. I don't see politics as right, left, or centre anymore. I see it as front-runners vs. rear-guarders. The rear-guard clings to old systems and structures, convinced they can hold back the tide. But they can't. The world is changing. Isn't it obvious?

Change doesn't happen in a straight line. It's messy. It's full of false starts, small wins, great leaps forward, and yes, sometimes a few steps backward. But resistance to change is a sign that something big is coming. It's the last gasp of the old order, desperately trying to hold on. Meanwhile, the undercurrent is shifting, and the future is being shaped beneath the surface. That's the magic of predictions. They're not about getting it right – they're about making us aware of the undercurrents. They prepare us for what's coming. They make us think, make us curious. And when we stop dismissing dreamers as dangerous idealists, maybe we'll start seeing the opportunities they see.

←#49

#49 The Risk Paradox

Navigating the tightrope between the old and the new? Risky. But here's the paradox: the more risks you take, the fewer you actually face. Sounds crazy, right? Well, let me walk you through it. I was at an event in Singapore a while back, and this other speaker – let's call him Mr Uncurious – had a real problem with this concept. He squinted at me and said, "So, you're telling me that by taking more risks, we actually take fewer risks? That sounds like a paradox." Yep, he wasn't wrong. It is a paradox, but like most paradoxes, it's all about perspective. By experimenting, by failing (yes, failing), we learn, we improve, and we reduce the risk of future mistakes.

But Mr. Uncurious wasn't done. "So we just throw everything on the line, fail gloriously, and then *poof* – magical success?" I smiled, stayed polite, and told him: it's about calculated risks. Yes, sometimes you fail. But failure isn't the end. It's a step. You learn, you grow, and you get better. But oh no, he still wasn't buying it. In his mind, failure = loss, period. What he didn't get was this: refusing to take risks? That's a guaranteed loss.

"Hmmm," he grumbled, "maybe you have a point, but curiosity as a KPI? That's a buzzword if I ever heard one. How do you even measure curiosity?" Ah, measuring curiosity – the classic scepticism. I assured him that it's doable. Curiosity is valuable because it drives innovation. It makes us ask better questions, learn more, and grow faster. His response? The dreaded "Yes, but..." He didn't get it. He thought curiosity was a fluffy excuse to take unnecessary risks. To him, curiosity meant running around like a kid at recess, throwing caution to the wind. But that's not it. Curiosity isn't recklessness; it's about daring to make mistakes and learn from them.

Still, Mr. Uncurious wasn't convinced. So, I shifted gears. I hit him with a different angle: talent. Curious people are drawn to places where they can grow. They want to learn, explore, and create. And if your organisation fosters that kind of environment, guess what? You attract top talent. "Oh, so now curiosity is a recruitment strategy?" he sneered. You bet it is. Curious people are the ones who bring fresh ideas and innovation. But he was still worried. "What if they ask too many questions? What if they take too many risks?" Translation: he didn't want to deal with mistakes. What he didn't get was that leaders need to create a space where mistakes aren't punished – they're learning moments. "Curiosity is too fluffy," he said, "too childish. Do you have more?"
Oh, do I ever. Curiosity helps companies make better decisions. High NCS companies make smarter choices about where to invest, when to pivot, and how to allocate resources. Cue Mr. Uncurious again: "Oh, so curiosity is also the key to strategy now? You really are obsessed with this stuff." Well, guilty as charged. I'm a fan of curiosity, and I make no apologies. But it's not some magic wand. It's a tool, a way of thinking that leads to better results.

He still wasn't sold, but guess what? He sat in on my keynote later that day – aptly titled *The Power of Curiosity*.

Navigating the space between old and new is tricky. But the more open you are to experimenting, the more you reduce the risks that come with change. And here's another fun paradox: avoiding risk altogether? That's the riskiest move you can make. Most companies? They avoid risk like it's their job. Their culture is all about safety, stability, and predictability. Experimentation? Nope. Too risky. But here's the truth: stagnation is riskier than change. By clinging to what's familiar, they miss opportunities. They fool themselves into thinking they're in control, but they're really just losing ground to competitors who are faster, more innovative, and more adaptive.

Avoiding risk leads to one outcome: irrelevance. The real risk is staying still while the world moves on. If you're not experimenting, not pushing boundaries, not making mistakes, you're falling behind. Sure, it feels safer, but it's a false sense of security. The companies that thrive? They're the ones that embrace the chaos, take risks, and treat failure as part of the process. The paradox is this: by taking more risks, they actually reduce the risks of becoming obsolete.

←#48 →Cycling Route Network 'Promoting Curiosity'

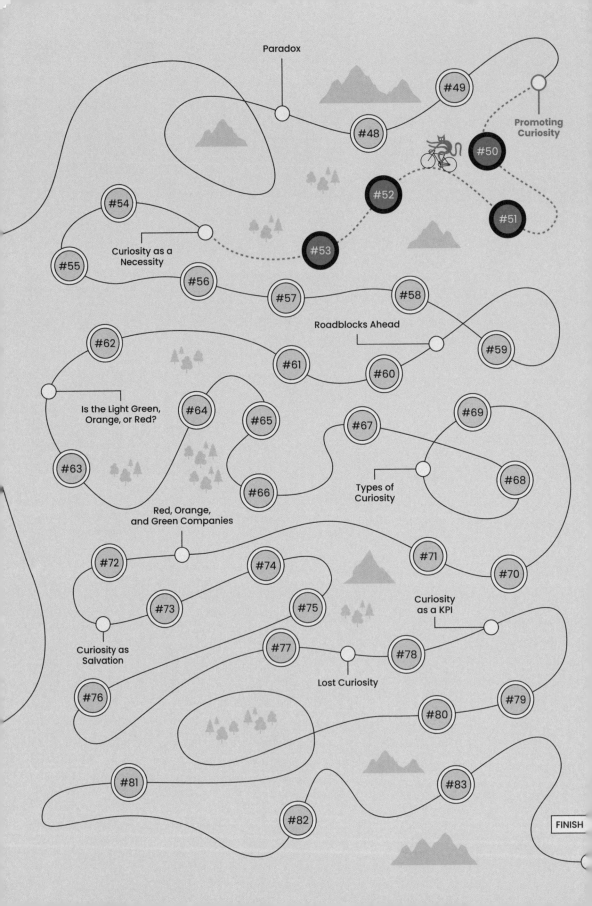

Cycling Route Network 'Promoting Curiosity'

First Steps

#50 How to begin

Dear Reader, I assume you're reading my book; otherwise, you wouldn't be here. You may have arrived at this point via a cycling node or simply by following the chapters linearly. I assume that by asking when the book would be available, you had additional questions you hoped would be answered here. Now, I have to guess those questions – a bit of a gamble, but one I'm willing to take. I imagine you're interested in actionable steps to build a culture of curiosity because you're convinced of its importance.

Let me refer you to the *Formula for Change* (←#27). The 'D' of *Things must change* is clear: the outside world is evolving rapidly, and you're facing a choice between missed opportunities or seized ones. The 'V' of 'Vision' is also clear: you want to cultivate curiosity. Keeping the *Formula for Change* in mind, and inspired by *The Martian* (←#40), you're ready to take that first step and want to know what it is. Well done! Here's how to foster a culture of curiosity:

Step 1: *Rethink the traditional hiring process.* Instead of focusing on filling existing roles or finding candidates who fit within a pre-existing blueprint, consider assessing the curiosity of potential new hires and making it a key factor in the hiring decision.

Step 2: *Design questions to gauge the candidate's curiosity.* In interviews, you could ask questions like:
- *Can you give an example of a time when you encountered a question or problem you didn't have an answer to, and how did you approach it?*

- How do you stay updated on new developments in your field?

Step 3: Consider using psychometric assessments, such as the *Five-Dimensional Curiosity Scale (5DC)* or the *Curiosity and Exploration Inventory-II (CEI-II)*, to provide an objective measure of a candidate's curiosity.

By prioritising curiosity in the hiring process, you can help foster a culture of curiosity within the organisation. Curious employees are often more engaged, creative, and better equipped to solve complex problems – all of which contribute to the long-term success of the organisation. It's important to emphasise that this doesn't mean other criteria, like experience or technical skills, aren't important. However, by viewing curiosity as a key factor, you can help create an environment where continuous learning and exploration are encouraged and valued.

This is an answer. Not *the* answer. That doesn't exist. It never does. Behind every answer lies a new question.

←#51

#51 The Wise Guru and the Business Leader: A Lesson in Curiosity

Let's be real – curiosity and strategy aren't exactly the yin and yang that most companies claim them to be. Oh, everyone *says* they're curious. They say they're all about innovation and forward-thinking. But come on, we both know that strategy is more of an art than a science. It's a precarious balancing act between gut instinct and hard data, between heart and mind. Curiosity? It's what keeps you from wobbling off that tightrope. Let me tell you a little story – a parable, if you will. And yes, any resemblance to a Coelho parable is purely coincidental. Promise.

One early morning, when the air was crisp enough to feel like tiny shards of ice hitting his lungs, a business leader set out on a quest. He climbed up a mountain, barefoot, with stones cutting into his feet, all to reach the high temple of a famous guru. No one knew the guru's name, but everyone knew his reputation – he was supposed to be a master not just of meditation, but of strategy. And this business leader? His company had hit a wall. Sure, they were still doing things sharper, faster, better – but the machine was starting to sputter. The gears were grinding, and no one knew why.

So, he trudged up the mountain, bleeding feet and all, to find the answers.

When he finally arrived, panting and half-dead, he spotted the guru sitting peacefully under an old, gnarled tree, meditating like he had all the time in the world. The business leader waited. Partly because, let's be honest, he needed to catch his breath. After a while, the guru opened his eyes and motioned for him to come closer. In a voice that was less like thunder and more like a whispering breeze, the guru asked, "What brings you to me with feet like those?"

"Master," the business leader wheezed, "I need advice on strategy. My company is at a crossroads. We've done everything we always do, only now... it's not working. I want to make sure that when we change, we're heading in the right direction."

The guru smiled, as gurus do, and pointed to a pond nearby – a mirror-like surface, perfectly still. "Look into the water," he said. "What do you see?"

The business leader hobbled over and gazed into the pond. "I see myself, Master," he muttered, grimacing. (*I'm getting old*, he thought.)

"Exactly," said the guru. "You see yourself. But look deeper. Beyond your reflection. What do you see now?"

Leaning in, the business leader stared harder. "I see stones at the bottom and little fish swimming around," he said, his voice cracking with what sounded a bit like... joy?

"Precisely," said the guru. "At first, you saw only the surface – yourself. But when you look deeper, you see what's hidden underneath. That's curiosity. It helps you see past the obvious, past the reflection, and into the deeper workings of things."

The business leader nodded, beginning to grasp the idea. "So, you're saying curiosity helps me see beyond the surface? That it lets me understand more than just what's staring back at me?"
"Indeed," the guru replied. "You want to know which direction to go. You think I can tell you. But how can you find your way if you've never started to walk? Curiosity is your compass. It guides you through the fog of uncertainty. It's not about knowing the destination – it's about exploring, about asking better questions. Only then will your strategy unfold."

"But Master," the business leader protested, "how does curiosity help me manage risks? It sounds like you're telling me to just wander around without a plan. Isn't that... unwise?"

The guru stood, walking to a nearby orchard. "Follow me," he said, "Don't worry, the grass is soft – it will heal your feet."

When they reached the trees, the guru plucked two apples. "Here," he said, holding them up. "These are both apples, but which one is sweeter?"

The business leader hesitated, confused. "I... I don't know, Master. I'd have to taste them first."

The guru smiled. "Exactly. If you don't take a bite, how will you know? That's what curiosity is. It's tasting both apples. It's the willingness to try, to explore, to learn. It lets you assess risks, figure out what's worth pursuing, and adapt as you go."

The business leader's eyes widened in understanding. "So curiosity isn't just a tool – it's part of the strategy itself. It helps me navigate the unknown, not recklessly, but intelligently."

"Precisely," said the guru, now practically glowing with wisdom (because, of course, he was). "Curiosity lets you see. It lets you uncover the meaning behind the data, behind the surface facts, and create strategies that actually work in the real world, not just on paper."

And with that, the guru sat back down under his tree, signalling the end of the conversation. The business leader thanked him, bowing deeply, and began his descent back down the mountain. As he walked, he felt lighter. Sure, his feet still hurt, but his mind was clearer. He now understood that curiosity wasn't a side note – it was the key to unlocking the full potential of his strategy. It was the spark that ignited innovation, the lens that revealed new possibilities, and the driving force behind learning, growing, and evolving. So, what's the takeaway? The guru's little parable shows us that curiosity isn't just about asking a

> few questions. It's about being open, being willing to explore, and – most importantly – being willing to taste both apples before making decisions. Curiosity is the compass that guides us through the unpredictable terrain of strategy, making it stronger, more resilient, and ready for whatever comes next.

←#50 →#52

#52 Attracting and Retaining Talent: The Role of Art and Creativity

A company that implements NCS can attract curious individuals – talents who love to learn, thrive on knowledge, and delight in exploration. These organisations aren't just a collection of employees; they are curiosity incubators. They create an environment where talent is not only drawn in but also nurtured and encouraged to flourish. These are the true architects of the future, who see cultivating curiosity not merely as a task but as a calling. They recognise that curious individuals don't just accumulate knowledge – they amplify the culture of curiosity itself. It's a double flywheel, a perpetual motion of intellectual growth.

Why, you may ask, is this so crucial? Because curious people, by their very nature, learn more, longer, and deeper. They are the explorers of the unknown, the pioneers of the impossible. They are the ones who ask questions others haven't even considered. This insatiable hunger for the unknown propels them to become extraordinary leaders. They are the leaders unafraid to challenge the status quo, who navigate the depths of complexity. They build bridges where others see only walls. Through their example, they inspire others to look beyond the surface, to dig deeper than the obvious.

In short, companies that cultivate curiosity are not only incubators of talent but also catalysts for progress. So, don't settle for what you know – strive for what you have yet to discover. As the great philosopher Socrates once said, "I know that I know nothing." In this acknowledgment lies true strength. Can you, as a leader, help to foster such an organisation? How do we cultivate curiosity in practice? Here are some concrete steps:

1. Ask questions yourself. By thinking out loud about things, we spark the curiosity of others. It's a simple but powerful way to create an environment of inquiry and discovery.
2. Ask open-ended questions. Avoid questions that can be answered with a simple yes or no. Instead, ask questions that begin with Why, How, What, Where, When, Who. This type of questioning invites deeper thinking and more elaborate answers.
3. Encourage curiosity and exploration. Foster an environment of collaboration and teamwork. Encourage your team members to share their ideas and help each other solve problems.
4. Integrate art and creativity. Embrace mistakes and celebrate failures. This helps promote a culture of risk-taking and innovation.
5. Learn creative problem-solving techniques. Provide time for reflection. This helps to develop a deeper understanding of problems and find new solutions.
6. Be a role model for creativity. Show your own curiosity and passion for learning. Your enthusiasm and dedication can inspire others to do the same.

Why, you ask, point 4, art? Well, you can use art and creative activities as tools to stimulate curiosity and innovative thinking. In the context of an organisation, this can mean creating space for creative projects or brainstorming sessions, where team members are encouraged to think outside the box and explore new ideas. This can also mean placing value on aesthetic considerations in the work we do, or creating room for artistic expression in the workplace. Furthermore, when I say "embrace mistakes and celebrate failures", I mean that we should recognise that mistakes and failures are often our best teachers. Rather than seeing them as negatives, we can view them as opportunities to learn and grow. By fostering a culture in which failures are celebrated, we encourage risk-taking and innovation.

←#51 #50 →#53

#53 Customer Loyalty, Customer-Focused and Customer-Centric

Perhaps it's time to recognise that real curiosity lies in discovering how we can improve ourselves and how the customer can help us in this endeavor. In today's world, the customer is no longer just a passive receiver of our products and services but an active participant in a mutually beneficial relationship. We know that curiosity works bidirectionally. If we wield curiosity as a 'weapon', then the relationship with the customer becomes a dance of mutual attraction. It is no longer a one-sided exploration, but a dynamic exchange in which both parties are actively involved.

When a company is genuinely curious about its customers and the person behind that customer or consumer, it asks questions that go beyond the obvious and therefore superficial needs. They dig deeper into desires, dreams, and daily challenges. This curiosity shows that they see the customer not just as a walking, living, breathing unfinished order but as an essential part of the ecosystem. (Yes, I'm sneaking in *The Guide to the Ecosystem* here, so you might (re)read that book, too.)

When customers feel they are at the centre of our attention, it creates a special sense of connection and trust. In the spotlight of curious attention, the customer, in turn, becomes curious about the companies showing this interest. The effect is reciprocal. Customers want to know more about who these companies are, what they offer, and whether their products and services can enrich their lives. This mutual curiosity creates a powerful dynamic that goes beyond traditional customer loyalty: it builds a relationship based on genuine interest and engagement. So, instead of focusing on how we can make customers loyal to us, we should concentrate on how we can create an environment where curiosity flows naturally in both directions. In this way, companies foster an environment in which customers are not only consumers but also co-creators, partners in an ongoing dialogue that shapes and enriches the company itself.

In this context, curiosity becomes not only a tool to promote customer loyalty but also a fundamental lever for business growth and innovation. Curiosity drives us to improve, to enhance our services, and to create products that not only meet customer needs but exceed them.

'Customer-oriented' is not the right approach; we should aim for 'customer-centric'. The concept of 'customer-oriented' sounds noble, but it misses the essence of what it truly means to operate in today's hyper-connected world. It suggests a passive attitude, where companies see themselves as entities that adapt to the customer rather than actively revolving around them. By staying 'oriented', companies still see themselves as the epicentre, while no one is the centre in a world where everything and everyone is connected, with everything and everyone being both sender and receiver. It's a crucial nuance we must not overlook.

In a 'customer-centric' approach, we place the customer at the radiant centre of all our activities. It's not about directing our services toward the customer, but about building our entire business structure, culture, and ethos with the customer as the foundation. In a customer-centric approach, every strategy, every product, every service is designed with the customer as the starting point. It's a dynamic, interactive process, where the customer not only provides feedback but also actively contributes to shaping the offerings. This is a world in which products and services are not created for the customer but with the customer.

This approach acknowledges that customers are more than just consumers: they are advisors, influencers, and even innovators. By placing them at the centre, we recognise their role in co-creating value. It's an acknowledgment that without the customer, there is no focal point around which companies can revolve. A customer-oriented approach can position a company as responsive and attentive, while a customer-centric approach transforms a company into an entity that truly lives and breathes *through* and *for* its customers. It represents a shift from a reactive attitude to a proactive collaboration, from following the customer to leading with the customer. Customer-oriented is a step in the right direction, but customer-centric brings about the true revolution. It's an approach that not only asks what we can do for the customer but, more importantly, what companies can achieve together with the customer.

←#52#51#50 →Cycling Route Network 'Curiosity as a Necessity'

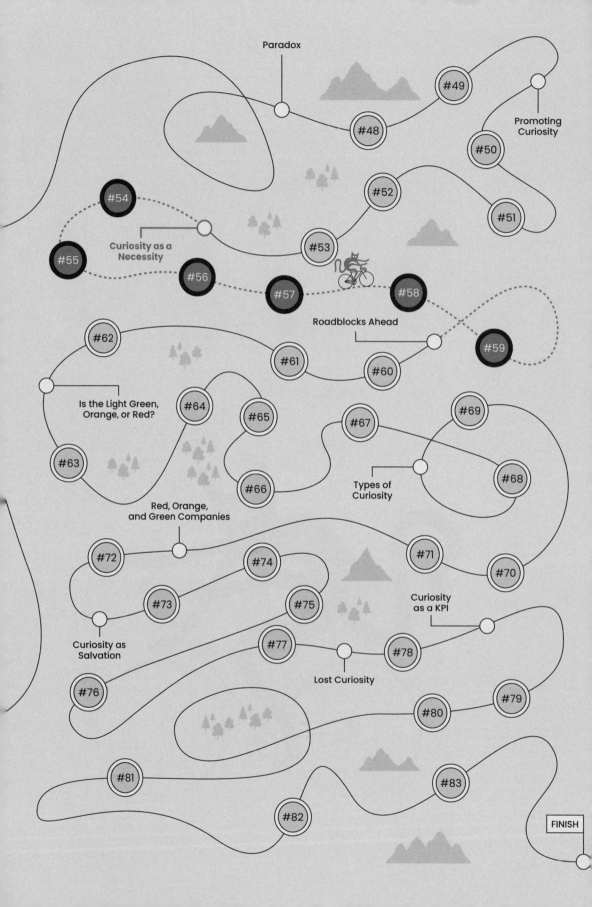

Cycling Route Network 'Curiosity as a Necessity'

#54 Curiosity is not a Luxury in the Twilight Twenties

Curiosity is a Compass. The 'Twilight Twenties' are an era of uncertainty. Curiosity is a valuable tool to navigate this zone of the unknown. A high NCS (Curiosity Score) can help companies remain flexible, ready to pivot at any moment in response to unforeseen challenges. In summary, the business case for implementing the NCS lies in its potential to drive innovation, increase employee engagement, gain customer insights, maintain a competitive advantage, manage risks, attract talent, make better strategic decisions, foster customer loyalty, and adapt to the ever-changing business environment of the 'Twilight Twenties'. Curiosity is no longer a luxury; it is a necessity for companies that aim for sustainability and growth.

A high NCS indicates a culture where questioning and exploration are encouraged, which is essential to stay agile and pivot quickly in response to unforeseen challenges. In the business world, curiosity translates into the ability to look beyond the horizon and discover opportunities where others see only risks. Curiosity drives innovation and creativity, which are crucial at a time when traditional business models and strategies are under pressure. The 'Twilight Twenties' demand a new approach to leadership and management, where curiosity is not only valued but also systematically embedded into the corporate culture. This means creating an environment where employees are encouraged to ask questions, conduct experiments, and learn from both successes and failures.

The NCS should therefore not only assess whether employees are curious but also whether the company fosters and is receptive to curiosity. As companies navigate this era of uncertainty, those that embrace curiosity will be the ones that not only survive but also thrive. They will be able to adapt, innovate, and grow quickly, no matter the challenges they encounter. Curiosity is more than a mental trait; it is a strategic tool that enables companies to navigate the unknown waters of the future. It is the driving force behind a new generation of business leaders and entrepreneurs willing to challenge the status quo and push the boundaries of what is possible.

←#55

#55 From Solution Selling to Curiosity as a Driver

For decades, sales has been a parade of buzzwords and trendy systems – each one hailed as the next big thing. Solution selling? The classic: "Don't sell the drill, sell the hole." It's 2024, and some are still pushing this as if it's new and revolutionary. Spoiler alert: it's not. And yet, every now and then, you hear another sales coach dragging it onto the stage like it's the answer to everything. Take Challenger Sales, Matt Dixon's approach – where you dig deep into the customer's needs and offer them insights they didn't even know they wanted. Sounds smart, right? And it is. But whether it's creating a problem for your solution or challenging your customer to rethink their needs, the whole game really boils down to one thing: curiosity.

Curiosity is what separates the average from the extraordinary salesperson. It's what gets you beyond the surface – past the SPANCOs and AIDAs of the world – and lets you actually get to know the person behind the customer. Understand them, stimulate them, reward them. Most salespeople? They rely on assumptions, thinking they know best. Funny, right? It's a little arrogant.

Let me tell you a story. I was once responsible for buying a fleet of vehicles. Big deal, right? So, one Saturday, I roll into the chosen supplier's showroom – jeans, T-shirt, unshaven. Invisible. Thirty minutes of wandering later, some sales guy finally approaches, checks his watch like I'm already wasting his day, and says, "I don't think you can afford this car, sir." His funeral. But I see this stuff all the time. Then there was the sales guru I had to follow on stage at a conference in France. She preached: "If they're in jeans, forget it. No sale." I stepped up next in Levi's and a T-shirt and said, "Thanks for ensuring I'll get zero help in your store."

Or how about the time I took my grandkids to a kitchen showroom? The salesperson, mid-sandwich, looked at us, looked at the kids, and said, "We sell expensive kitchens here, sir. You might want to look elsewhere." Another genius. And then there was the sailboat photo in my office. No one asked if I actually liked sailing (I don't). But somehow, every salesperson assumed I was a sailor and used that as their opening line. Less than 10% of them bothered to ask first. Most just skipped curiosity entirely, operating on assumptions.

Curiosity is the key. You have to dig. You have to care. It's not the latest method that makes the difference – it's how curious you are about the person in front of you. That's where the real value comes in.

←#54 →#56

#56 Sell the Pen

"Why don't you tell your salespeople to be curious?"

Here's why: because you're telling them to sell, sell a lot, and sell it at the highest price possible. Curiosity? That's fluff. You've got rainmakers to make money, and their bonuses depend on it. Here's the game: more sales, bigger margins, faster. Hard to argue with that, right? Except... you've got them chasing the prey so hard, they don't stop to see the context.

Let's play a little role-playing game. You're in a room. I've got two groups of salespeople – Group A and Group B. Group A? They've got one mission: sell you a luxury pen in ten minutes for the highest price possible. Time is money. Group B? They get a different mission: learn as much as they can about you in ten minutes. Be curious.

Group A? They're working every angle, every sales trick in the book. They're trying to sell you the pen even if you already have a drawer full of them. Each one is out for bragging rights: who sold the priciest pen, who closed the fastest. It's a snake pit.

Group B? They get a pen too – but to write. And they're told to ask questions. Find out who you are, what you love, where you're from. Ten minutes later, they're comparing stories, sharing what they learned.

Now, you're thinking: *Great, but where's the sale?* Aren't salespeople supposed to sell? Hold up. Here's the follow-up. I bring in a bunch of random objects – pens, notebooks, coffee machines, whiteboard markers. I ask both groups to come up with a plan to sell you as many of these objects as possible. Group A? Chaos. Group B? Strategy. They're nuanced, they know you, and they'll sell more. Including that pen.

← #55 #54 → #57

#57 Curiosity as a Powerful Marketing Tool

There's a company that holds its cards so close to its chest that the whole world is on the edge of their seat, begging for the next reveal. That company is Apple. Their product launches are masterpieces – just enough mystery to get people's curiosity spinning, but not enough to give the game away. And when they finally drop the big reveal? Boom – people are hooked. It's not just Apple. Tesla does the same. Back when Elon Musk still had both feet on the ground (2013-2020, let's say), Tesla's product reveals were the stuff of legend. The Cybertruck with its shattering glass? Marketing gold. Launching a Roadster into space? Who does that? Musk, that's who.

Why don't more companies do this? Simple: it takes discipline and patience. It's about building long-term anticipation rather than chasing short-term profits. When used right, curiosity is one of the most powerful marketing tools out there. Apple, Tesla – they're proof that curiosity, combined with innovation and storytelling, turns a brand into a legend.

I'll give you an example. I was at a Tesla supercharger station in Amsterdam, just minding my own business. Suddenly, the place is packed. Champagne. Big screens. People glued to their phones. What's going on? Musk was announcing the Model 3 – no billboards, no commercials. Just curiosity doing all the heavy lifting. And then? Tesla announces the order numbers. The whole world is speechless. Traditional automakers? They're in a panic, realising their expensive marketing campaigns and showrooms were no longer their biggest assets but their biggest burdens. Curiosity drives engagement. Musk took a page from Steve Jobs' playbook and added his own spin. No huge marketing budget, just a relentless focus on building a better product – and letting curiosity do the rest.

←#56#55#54 →#58

#58 Communicating Vessels: Successful Innovation, Marketing, and Profit

Innovation is the engine of a company. It's not just about cranking out shiny new products – it's about capturing attention. Companies like Tesla don't need billboards. They innovate so much, their products practically market themselves. (←#57) On the flip side, companies that don't innovate? They have to throw more cash into marketing just to stay relevant. It's a constant juggle between creating something new and shouting about it from the rooftops. But here's the thing: marketing and innovation shouldn't be two separate forces. They should work together.

Here's how: Marketing gives you the juicy feedback you need to make your product better. Meanwhile, innovation gives marketing something worth talking about – a unique selling point that stands out. It's a dance. Innovation shouldn't just be about flashy tech. It's about creating a story that hits home. And marketing? Well, marketing needs to tell that story so people feel it.

At the core of all this? Curiosity. Curiosity leads to better products, which means you need less traditional marketing. Curiosity is what gets consumers hooked. You don't need gimmicks when people are genuinely intrigued. When curiosity drives both innovation and marketing, your message spreads like wildfire. You tease just enough to spark the imagination and leave people wanting more. Invest in innovation, fuel curiosity, and watch your marketing costs shrink while your profits grow.

←#57#56#55#54 →#59

#59 The Curious See the Hyperconnected Network Society

Traditional companies? They're stuck in the old days of radio, TV, and billboards. They broadcast their messages and cross their fingers that someone's listening. But guess what? They're talking at people, not with people. Visionaries like Steve Jobs and Elon Musk? They got it. They knew that in today's hyperconnected network society, communication isn't a monologue – it's a conversation. Jobs and Musk understood that you can't just toss out a message and hope for the best. You've got to engage in a lively, two-way exchange. Traditional companies? They just keep pumping out the same old mass communication. Meanwhile, Jobs and Musk opened up a dialogue, creating communities where consumers felt like they were part of something bigger.

By harnessing the power of the internet and social media, these companies created feedback loops. That's the magic sauce – constant product improvement driven by real-time input from their audience. And they did it at viral speed, with no borders or barriers. Curiosity became a viral tool. Content that sparks curiosity gets shared. A lot. It creates emotional connections, and when you've got emotions in play, you've got engagement.

Traditional companies? They're still struggling to figure out how this works. They're slow to adapt, clinging to outdated communication strategies while their more hyperconnected competitors leave them in the dust. If you want to thrive in this new era, you've got to evolve. Start a dialogue, embrace feedback, and let curiosity be your guide.

←#58#57#56#55#54 →Cycling Route Network 'Roadblocks Ahead'

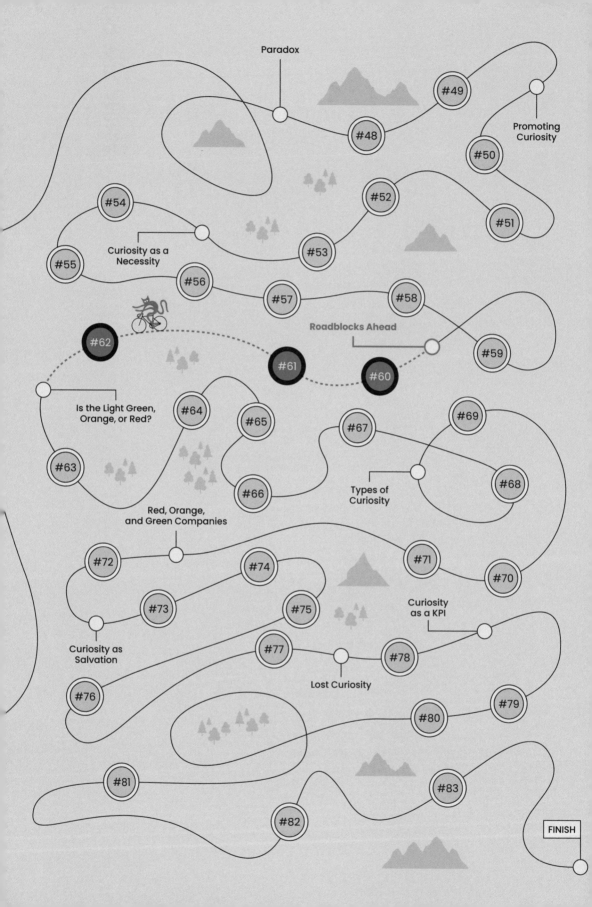

Cycling Route Network 'Roadblocks Ahead'

#60 Established, Conservative, the Right Balance

Curiosity? It makes employees question everything. They find better ways, take smarter risks, and keep the company on its toes. But for traditional companies like Nestlé and Unilever? Curiosity might sound a little... dangerous. These are brands built on consistency, not mystery. Their products are essentials – the stuff of everyday life. So, the question becomes: How much curiosity can you really inject into a bar of chocolate or a bottle of shampoo?

Sure, curiosity-driven marketing is sexy. But it's also risky. It needs a dash of secrecy and a sprinkle of surprise. And for established brands, playing it safe has worked for decades. Why mess with that? After all, they've got a well-oiled machine, with marketing campaigns that are dependable, if not exactly thrilling. Why take risks when what you've got works?

That said, even the most conservative brands can benefit from a little curiosity. The key is balance. You can't just rip a page from Jobs' or Musk's playbook and expect it to work for you. It has to fit with your culture, your customers, and your story. Dive into curiosity too fast, and you could end up losing control of the message. Once something goes viral, it's out there, and it's not always going to do what you want. The answer? Authenticity. Be real. Be transparent. Consumers can smell inauthenticity a mile away. Find the right balance between tradition and innovation, and don't leap into the trend pool just because everyone else is. Take your time. Be curious, but be careful.

←#59#58#57#56#55#54 →#61

#61 Recommendations

So, we've reached that part of the book where I give you the highlights. I know some of you are leaning in, thinking, "Finally! The quick fix! The answers all neatly packaged and bullet-pointed." I see you. You're the checklist lover. And that's fine.

But before you start patting yourself on the back, let's pause for a moment. Did you really need to fast-forward here? Could you have skipped all the messy, thought-provoking, curiosity-stoking stuff we've covered? I mean, sure, some might call this section a shortcut, while others will see it as the moment they've been waiting for – finally, some handles to grab onto. Well, guess what? I've tried to keep this juicy enough for both camps. You'll get your overview... but with a little spice.

Why Measure NCS (Net Curiosity Score)?

- **Innovation and Adaptation:**
  - The 'Twilight Twenties' are unpredictable – curiosity fuels innovation and adaptability.
- **Employee Engagement:**
  - Curious employees are more engaged. Simple.
- **Customer Insights:**
  - Curiosity digs deep into customer needs.
- **Competitive Advantage:**
  - Stay ahead by curiously exploring trends.
- **Risk Mitigation:**
  - A higher NCS means a greater willingness to take calculated risks.

- **Attracting and Retaining Talent:**
  - Curious people want to be part of curious companies. No brainer.
- **Strategic Decision-Making:**
  - More curiosity = smarter decisions.
- **Customer Loyalty:**
  - Innovate continuously, and you'll keep customers loyal.
- **Adapting to the Unknown:**
  - Curiosity is your guide through the unknown.
- **The Business Case for NCS:**
  - Stimulates innovation. Boosts engagement. Minimises risk. Brings talent. Satisfies customers.

Applying Apple and Tesla's Curiosity Marketing to Your Business:
1. Create Anticipation: Tease them with sneak peeks and cryptic hints.
2. Craft a Story: Don't just sell – tell.
3. Live Demos: Engage people by showing, not just telling.
4. User-Centred Design: Focus on how the product fits into their life.
5. Leverage Social Media: Build a community that promotes your brand.
6. Direct Sales Approach: Cut out the middleman where possible.
7. Focus on Digital: Create a solid digital marketing strategy.
8. Target the Right Audience: Know who you're talking to.
9. Innovate and Embrace Competition: Stay bold and welcome a little friendly competition.

Why Curiosity Works as a Marketing Tool:
1. Mystery and Anticipation:
   - People love solving puzzles. Tease their brains.
2. Surprise and Delight:
   - Catch them off guard with something they didn't see coming.
3. Cultivating Loyalty:
   - Build a community that loves to talk about you.

4. Storytelling and Emotion:
   - Make your product relatable, not just functional.
5. Tesla's Edge:
   - Disrupt the market by making people curious about the future.

Why Traditional Companies Hesitate with Curiosity Marketing:
- Brand Consistency: They stick to the tried and true.
- Broad Audience: Their products are aimed at everyone, so no surprises here.
- Essential Products: No room for mystery when you're selling toothpaste.
- Risk Aversion: Playing it safe has worked for them. Until it doesn't.
- Long Marketing Traditions: They've done it the same way for decades.
- Resource Allocation: They'd rather put their money elsewhere.
- Market Position: They're already at the top... for now.

Why Be Cautious with Viral Curiosity:
- Loss of Control: Once it's out there, it's gone. Beware.
- Reputation Risk: Viral doesn't always mean good.
- Rapid Response Needed: Be ready to respond fast.
- Authenticity Rules: Consumers can smell fake from a mile away.
- Resource-Intensive: It's not cheap to stay on top of the game.
- Strategy Required: Align your curiosity with your brand's values, or else.

And there you have it. Whether you're here for the deep dive or just the TL;DR version, we're covering both ends of the spectrum. But remember, curiosity isn't just a side dish – it's the main course. Time to take these recommendations and run with them, whichever camp you're in.

←#60#59#58#57#56#55#54 →#62

#62 Brakes On? Framing

You know how it goes. Curiosity is awesome until it isn't – until someone says, "Wait a minute, shouldn't this be aligned with our goals?" There's always a little pushback, isn't there? Sure, curiosity boosts engagement, but don't get too curious or you'll lose focus. Innovation is great, but only if it adds value, they say. Adaptability? Important, but not too much. God forbid things change too fast. And personal growth? Just don't outgrow the company. Oh, and a positive work environment? Yeah, but let's not get too cosy – it might become an echo chamber where only the popular ideas survive. Can't have that.

And yes, social connections at work are valuable – but let's not get cliquey, okay? Balance, balance, balance. Curiosity is good... but with the right focus, right? Here's the real question though: what if those old goals don't cut it anymore in this new world that's emerging? Why are we so eager to carefully manage curiosity when it's precisely the untamed hunger for knowledge that leads to the best breakthroughs? There are two types of curiosity, and this is where it gets juicy: exploratory curiosity – the wild child that drives us into uncharted territory, the urge to discover what lies beyond the horizon. This is where the magic happens. And then there's goal-directed curiosity – the more buttoned-up sibling. This is where we dig deeper to solve specific problems, guided by an insatiable thirst for understanding. Both are necessary. Both are beautiful.

The business world needs this balance. The exploratory curiosity that says, "Let's see what's out there," and the goal-directed kind that says, "Now, how do we use what we've found?" Most businesses live and die by the latter. But ignore the former, and you'll miss the entire point of innovation.

←#61#60#59#58#57#56#55#54 →Cycling Route Network 'Is the Light Green, Orange, or Red?'

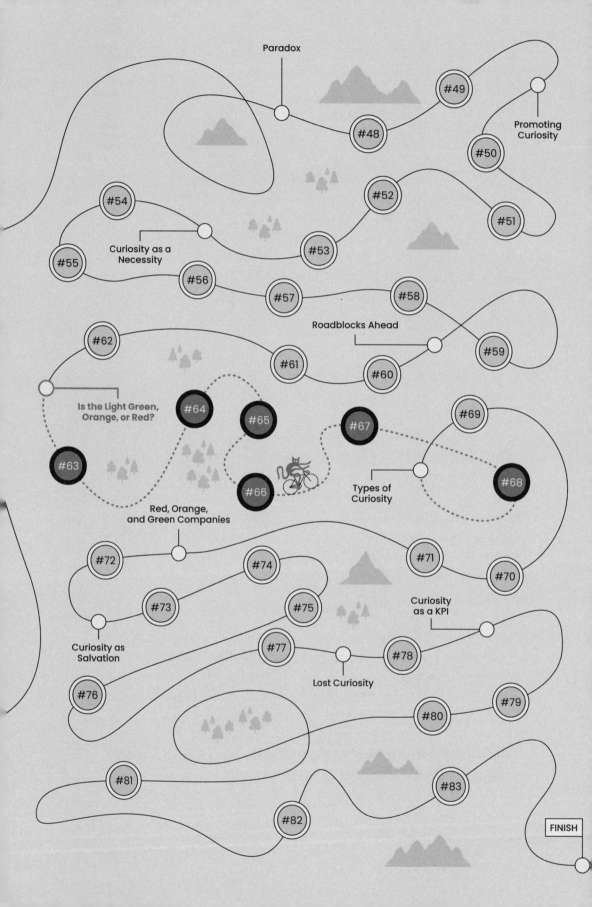

Cycling Route Network
'Is the Light Green, Orange, or Red?'

#63 Three Boxes on a Beach, Part 1

Let's take a little trip to 2022. I'm leading a four-hour session on innovation in a castle. Yep, a real one. It's for a company from Ghent. Now, to make this session a bit more punchy, I whipped up a framework – on the spot, mind you – that extends my beach chair analogy. Because, let's face it, innovation isn't about sitting on the beach polishing chairs while the real action is out on the ocean.

The business leader doesn't always need to be the one surfing those waves, but somebody does. You can't all be beachside, managing operations, while the big waves pass you by. So, I introduce three boxes on the beach: green, orange, and red. I quickly turn it into a mini-workshop, and lo and behold, it sticks. It's now a staple of my keynotes. Some companies have even turned these concepts into physical rooms – rooms where the innovation magic happens.

Innovation needs structure. You can't just send your best surfers out and hope they bring back something useful. No, you need a system to gather, evaluate, and act on what they find. That's where the three boxes come in. Green, orange, red. Colour-coded innovation – who knew?

←#64

#64 Three Boxes on a Beach, Part 2

All right, let's break it down.

Green Box

This is where you put the waves that are barely ripples on the horizon. They're small, insignificant, but – pay attention – they're there. Green box waves are things you keep an eye on. You don't have to act on them yet. Just... watch. This is the box where ideas can sit for years until suddenly, they grow into something bigger. Companies that miss opportunities usually forget to keep their green box in sight. They probably saw the wave five years ago but didn't think it was worth tracking. Big mistake.

Example? AI. If companies had put AI in their green box a decade ago, they wouldn't be panicking now. Same with electric cars. Tesla wasn't the first to the party, but when Musk showed up, traditional automakers should have moved that technology from the green to the amber box. They didn't. Whoops.

Orange Box

These waves are growing. You can feel it. They're not quite tsunamis yet, but they're worth surfing. The trick? Deciding fast. Once these waves reach their tipping point, you either catch them or you don't. You have to know when to jump on and when to back off. If you ride a wave too long and it fizzles out, you've wasted time. But if you miss a massive one – well, good luck explaining that to the shareholders.

Red Box

This is the box of regret. The missed waves. You didn't surf it, and now you're standing on the beach, watching others ride it while you scramble to save what's left of your sandcastle. And sometimes, it's worse than just missing the wave. Sometimes, the wave is a tsunami, and your entire business gets wiped out. Companies that didn't move AI into the amber box five years ago? They're looking at a red box moment right now. Panic on the beach, and everyone's shouting, "If only we had acted back then!" Yep, too late.

←#63 →#65

#65 The Three Boxes, Part 3

The exercise is deceptively simple: fill the boxes. Three waves in the green box, three in the amber, three in the red. Easy, right? Wrong. Here's what always happens:
1. Lively discussions break out within groups. People love to argue over where things belong.
2. The outcomes are all over the place. What one group puts in the green box, another shoves into red – and they're all from the same company.
3. Over time, you see shifts. One team's red becomes the next team's amber, and so on.
4. Most people say, "I've never thought about the future like this before." It's both hard work and a discovery process.

It's not about being right or wrong. It's about getting into the habit of thinking this way. The process itself is more important than the outcome. And I love it when participants get frustrated – because that's when they realise how much they haven't been thinking about the future.

After the initial frustration fades, I hit them with two more questions:
1. How do you keep the green box full and diverse?
2. When do you pull something from green to amber? When do you move from observation to action?

Suddenly, they realise they need clearer guidelines. But guess what? I don't provide them. This isn't paint-by-numbers. They've felt the pain, now they need to craft the solutions.

←#64 #63 →#66

#66 An Essential Part of the Three-Box Method

The green box is the unsung hero of the three-box method. It's where companies learn to stay alert. It's where you collect all those tiny trends that could one day become the next big thing. If you're not filling your green box, you're not really preparing for the future.
In all the times I've run this exercise, the same suggestions for filling the green box keep popping up:
- Tech newsletters and following thought leaders to stay ahead of emerging technologies.
- Partnering with sociologists or trend watchers to understand cultural shifts.
- Hosting "surfer meetings" where teams discuss trends and ideas.
- Listening deeply to customer feedback. Sometimes the biggest insight comes from the smallest complaint.
- Building a diverse network. Connect with people outside your bubble for cross-pollination of ideas.

The key to keeping the green box filled? Curiosity. Companies that don't cultivate curiosity are already behind. Innovation doesn't come from sitting around waiting for the future to happen. It comes from actively looking for it. Curiosity keeps you ahead of the game. It's the secret sauce for turning a ripple into a wave. The companies that succeed are the ones who think like surfers – always watching the horizon, always ready to paddle out when they see something worth catching.

> *Fostering a culture of curiosity, in which employees are encouraged to thinking outside the box and all share ideas among themselves that challenge the tatus quo challenge even if these ideas be unconventional.*

←#65 #64 #63 →#67

#67 The Realm of Opportunities: The Orange Box

I love the colour amber – the middle of the traffic light. It's not quite go and not quite stop. It's that sweet spot where you can still make your move. And that's where the amber box lives – right in the zone of opportunity. I often say I wish companies were more amber and less red. Here's the truth: red is reactive. It's catch-up. It's too late. When you're in the red, you're scrambling. Amber is proactive. It's where curiosity gets a chance to turn into action, before you're forced into it.

The problem? Companies are naturally resistant to change. They wait too long, and suddenly not changing is the biggest risk of all. Enter the Formula for Change (←#27). Companies resist change until it becomes a burning platform, and by then, it's too late.

The only force that naturally pushes against this resistance is curiosity. But we've unlearned that. We've killed it. We say "curiosity killed the cat" (←#28), but what it really killed was our ability to see change coming before it's too late. Companies that aren't curious by default end up in the red.

And here's something that just hit me while writing this: orange is the colour of curiosity. It's the colour of creativity, enthusiasm, and adventure. It's the colour of youthful energy – that same youthful curiosity we abandon as we get older. In marketing, it's the colour that conveys fun and exploration. So, here's my message: become an orange company. Be curious. Be proactive. Don't wait until you're drowning in red.

←#66#65#64#63 →#68

#68 The Three-Box Method Revisited

In all my research on curiosity, I kept coming back to the Three-Box Method. It's simple, but it gets to the heart of the matter: observation, experimentation, and reactive innovation. Here's the rundown:

1. Green Box: This is your sandbox, your playground for new trends, technologies, concepts – everything that's on the horizon but doesn't demand action. It's where you put all those things you're not sure about yet. You observe. No pressure. No action required. It's just about keeping your eyes open.
2. Orange Box: Now, we're talking. The orange box is where you start playing with the stuff from the green box. You experiment, test, and explore. Maybe there's something here, maybe not. But if you don't experiment, you'll never know. The green feeds the amber, and the amber fuels the green. Without both, your red box will fill up fast.
3. Red Box: This is where the waves you missed live. Missed trends. Missed technologies. Missed opportunities. These are the things that have now turned into threats or regrets. And what's left? Reactive innovation, the kind where you're chasing the wave instead of riding it.

The real trick? Getting stuff from green to orange before it's too late. And the way to do that is to keep curiosity alive. If your green box is empty, your future is looking a bit bleak.

← #67 #66 #65 #64 #63 → Cycle route network 'Species curiosity'

Cycling Route Network 'Is the Light Green, Orange, or Red?'

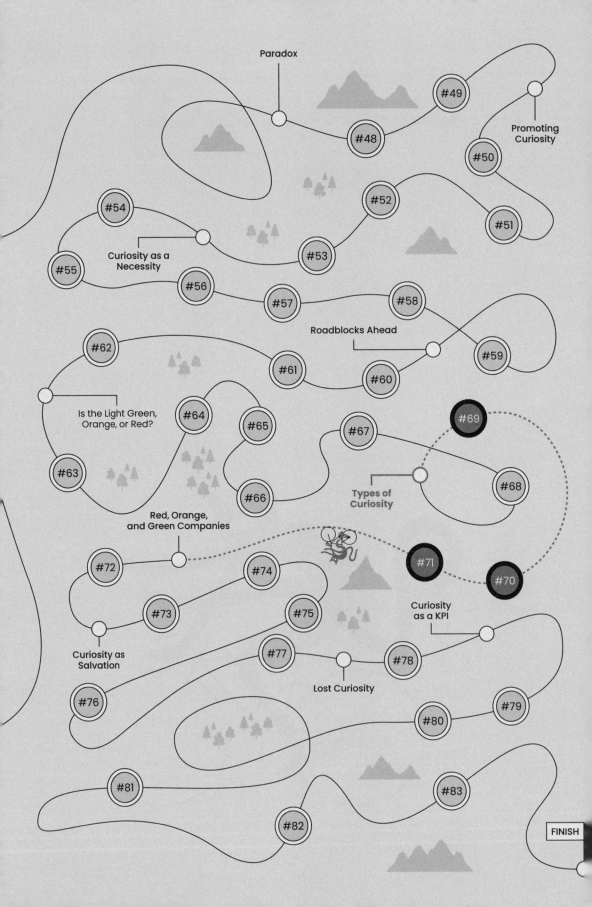

Cycling Route Network 'Types of Curiosity'

#69 Curiosity in Flavours with Todd Kashdan

Psychologist Todd Kashdan did a deep dive into curiosity, and what he found is fascinating. He broke curiosity down into two major categories (exploratory and specific), but later expanded into five distinct flavours. Let's break it down:

1. Sensory Curiosity: This is the desire for new sensory experiences – new sights, smells, tastes, textures. It's why we crave new foods, new music, new experiences. It's the starting point for a lot of creativity.
2. Cognitive Curiosity: The drive to solve puzzles, to understand complex problems, and to know how things work. This is the fuel behind lifelong learning.
3. Epistemological Curiosity: This is curiosity's deeper, philosophical side. The quest for knowledge about the universe, life, and human nature. It's what drives science and innovation.
4. Social Curiosity: This is all about understanding people – their stories, their behaviour. It's the curiosity that helps us build relationships and empathise with others. This type of curiosity creates great managers and team leaders.
5. Thrill-Seeking Curiosity: Think adrenaline junkies. It's the curiosity that makes someone jump out of an airplane, launch a car into space (thanks, Elon), or take massive risks to see what happens next.

While all five types are interesting, for this book, I've focused on just two: exploratory and specific. These are simple, straightforward, and, frankly, get the job done in a business context. Why? Because exploratory curiosity is what gets you out there, scanning the horizon, filling that green box. And specific curiosity is what helps you make sense of what you find, moving those trends into the orange box for action.

←#70

Exploratory, empathetic and specific

#70 Three Types of Curiosity

After all the digging and research, I boiled curiosity down to three main types:
1. Exploratory Curiosity – This is the classic thirst for knowledge. It's the search for new insights, new skills, and new ways of thinking. It's what makes employees want to learn, innovate, and stay ahead of the game. Think of it as the constant scanning of the horizon for the next big thing. Exploratory curiosity keeps your green box filled (←#68). It's the lifeblood of innovation because it pushes you to constantly adapt, experiment, and explore new trends.
2. Empathic Curiosity – This one's all about understanding people. It's the curiosity that drives you to ask, "What's really going on in someone's mind?" For customer-focused businesses, empathic curiosity is gold. It encourages employees to listen to their customers, understand their needs, and connect on a deeper level. It's what makes products and services truly resonate with people, not just function.
3. Specific Curiosity – This is the hyper-focused type. It's triggered by specific problems or questions that need deep exploration. This is what turns good enough into great. Specific curiosity leads to thorough, expert-level understanding in particular areas, making it crucial for perfecting processes, diving deep into product development, or mastering a niche market.

These three types of curiosity are the driving forces behind innovation and adaptability. When you cultivate all three, your organisation becomes a powerhouse of new ideas, empathy, and expertise. You're not just keeping up with trends – you're leading them.
Potential quotes:
- "Exploratory curiosity keeps you looking ahead; specific curiosity gets the job done."

- "Empathic curiosity connects you with the customer of tomorrow."
- "Curiosity doesn't just solve problems – it anticipates them."

←#69 →#71

#71 Open Perceptual Loops

In my earlier books, I encouraged businesses to look forward, always evolving. With this book, I've zeroed in on threefold curiosity as the most powerful engine for continuous evolution. The concept of open perceptual loops is about keeping curiosity alive and kicking in your organisation. It's about never closing the book – always asking questions, always learning, always improving.

Here's the beauty of open perceptual loops: they keep your organisation agile. When curiosity is encouraged, employees are driven to ask the right questions, experiment with new ideas, and avoid stagnation. It's about fostering an environment where everyone's on a quest for more – more knowledge, more innovation, more understanding of the market. Open perceptual loops drive continuous improvement in key areas:
- Employees constantly evolve – Knowledge never stays static. Employees are always learning, updating skills, and adapting.
- Innovation becomes the norm – By experimenting and not fearing failure, companies can stay ahead of change.
- Customer satisfaction skyrockets – Empathic curiosity leads to deeper insights into customer needs, creating products that truly meet those needs.

Incorporating exploratory, empathic, and specific curiosity into these loops allows a company to thrive in the face of rapid change.

←#70#69 →Cycling Route Network 'Red, Orange, and Green Companies'

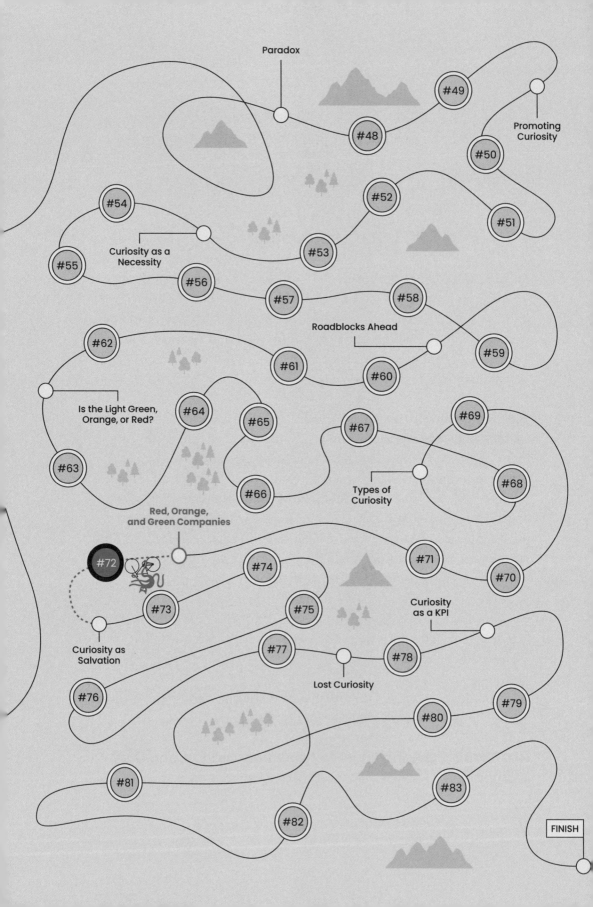

Cycling Route Network
'Red, Orange, and Green Companies'

#72 Checklist : Red, Orange, and Green Companies

In this checklist, I've adapted an exercise from my earlier work to help companies see where they stand on the curiosity spectrum:

1. Red Companies – These are the dinosaurs, stuck in the past, clinging to the status quo. They ignore curiosity, innovation, and forward-thinking. Employees may be curious, but the company culture stifles them. These companies aren't focused on tomorrow's customer – they're too busy trying to keep today's afloat.
2. Green Companies – These are the trailblazers. They live and breathe curiosity, constantly innovating and staying close to their customers. Their green box is always full, and their amber box is their playground for new experiments. They're nimble, proactive, and always one step ahead.
3. Orange Companies – These are in transition. They're trying to shift from red to green but haven't fully embraced curiosity yet. They see the need for change but are still figuring out how to get there.

Quick Self-Assessment:
1. Do you know your customer better than you know your own product?
2. Does your management think in terms of limitations or opportunities?
3. Is your leadership based on control or trust?
4. Are you hunting for customers to fit your product, or are you building products for your customers?
5. Are you driven by assumptions or curiosity?
6. Are your processes set in stone, or are they fluid and open to questioning?
7. Do you strive for perfection or allow room for failure?
8. Do you obsess over details or focus on the big picture?

9. Is tomorrow just an extension of today, or is it a whole new adventure?
10. Are your KPIs inwardly focused, or are they driven by external trends and customer needs?

This checklist provides companies with a snapshot of their curiosity health. Where do you fall? Red, orange, or green? The answer could decide your company's future.

→Cycling Route Network 'Curiosity as Salvation'

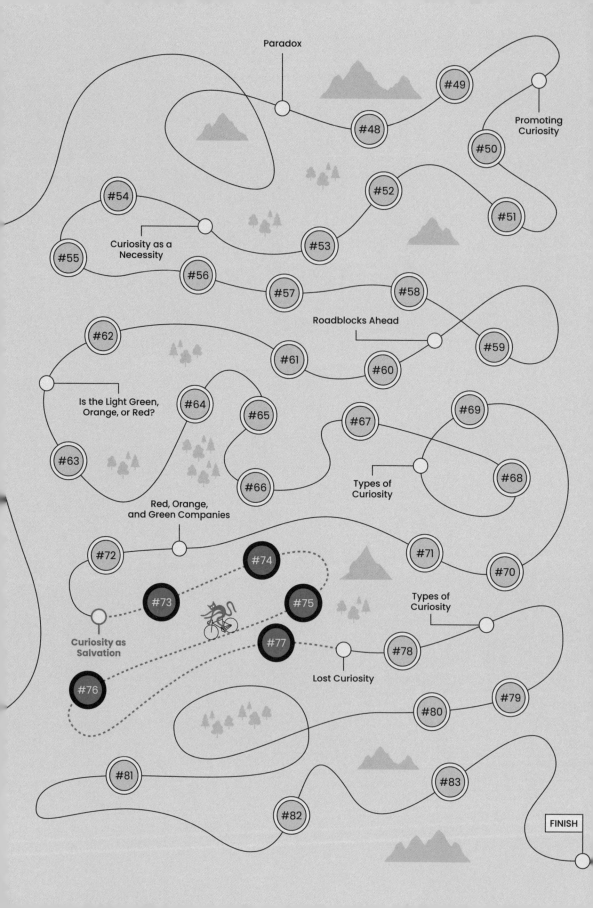

Cycling Route Network 'Curiosity as Salvation'

#73 What We Don't Know: Wicked Problems

In this Twilight Zone between crumbling old paradigms and new ones struggling to emerge, companies are facing their biggest existential questions: Will we still be relevant by 2030? By 2040? The answer is far from certain. The challenges ahead are massive, and they're not your run-of-the-mill problems. These are *wicked problems*. We've discussed them before in *The Guide to The Ecosystem Economy*, and they are the kinds of challenges that require companies to fundamentally rethink how they operate.

Wicked problems are complex, messy, and elusive. They don't come with clear-cut solutions or well-defined boundaries. They're nothing like the tidy, solvable, tame problems that engineers, accountants, and most MBA grads are trained to tackle. Tame problems have clear definitions, specific solutions, and measurable outcomes. Wicked problems? They laugh at your neat little spreadsheets. Here's what makes wicked problems stand out:

- No clear definition: You can't even fully define the problem, because it looks different depending on who's looking at it.
- No stop rule: There's no clean endpoint where you can declare victory. Wicked problems are often symptoms of deeper issues.
- No right or wrong answers: Solutions aren't clear-cut; they're more like 'better or worse', and the better is often subjective.
- Unique: Each wicked problem is a one-of-a-kind puzzle. No standard playbook can solve it.
- Delayed feedback: You won't know if your solution worked immediately. Consequences unfold slowly and often in unpredictable ways.
- Consequences ripple: Every action has unintended side effects, and those side effects can spawn new problems.

To face wicked problems, traditional problem-solving methods won't cut it. Instead, they require a holistic, collaborative approach, drawing in diverse perspectives and a willingness to iterate continuously.

> *What would people miss if your company with its services and products were no longer there? Now and in the future?*

→ #74

#74 Curiosity to the rescue

When it comes to managing wicked problems, curiosity is your secret weapon. These problems aren't going away with a formula or a checklist. You need curiosity to dig deep, think creatively, and rally the right minds. Here's how curiosity steps in to save the day:
- Uncovering root causes: Instead of slapping a Band-Aid on symptoms, curiosity pushes you to ask, "Why? Why? Why?" until you get to the heart of the issue.
- Generating creative solutions: Wicked problems don't have obvious solutions. Curiosity sparks that out-of-the-box thinking necessary to spot opportunities no one else has considered.
- Encouraging interdisciplinary collaboration: Wicked problems touch every corner of society. Curious minds bring together diverse perspectives, blending knowledge from fields that don't usually cross paths.
- Promoting continuous adaptation: There's no final answer. You need to be flexible, always learning from what's working and what isn't.
- Engaging stakeholders: Wicked problems affect a lot of people, and everyone's got a stake in the outcome. Curiosity fosters engagement, ensuring people stay involved and investedCuriosity is more

than just a nice trait to have; it's a strategic necessity for tackling these complex issues. A curious culture makes your team nimble, adaptive, and ready to face the unknown head-on.

←#73 →#75

#75 Three Scenarios in the Twilight Zone

In this Twilight Zone, three potential futures await us: collapse, plateau, or transcendence. The way we handle wicked problems will decide which of these we land in.

Collapse

If we fail to solve wicked problems, we're headed straight for collapse. Here's what that looks like:
- Reactive firefighting: Problems are only addressed when they become crises, with no long-term thinking.
- Escalation of issues: Wicked problems don't go away – they just evolve into bigger, scarier monsters.
- Systemic failure: When one part of the system collapses, it triggers a domino effect, taking everything down with it.

Plateau

Maybe we'll manage to hold things together just enough to avoid disaster, but we won't be making much progress either. This is the plateau scenario:
- Temporary fixes: We throw band-aids at the problem, just enough to keep things running but without solving the underlying issues.
- Stability, but no growth: We're not collapsing, but we're not thriving either.
- Limited innovation: We make small tweaks here and there, but nothing big enough to really move the needle.

Transcendence

The ideal outcome: transcendence. This is where we not only solve wicked problems but leap beyond them to build something better.
- Breakthrough innovation: We use wicked problems as the launchpad for radical new ideas.
- Systemic change: We transform the way we operate, building systems that can handle complexity and uncertainty.
- Future-focused: Instead of just surviving, we thrive by imagining and building a future that's more than we ever thought possible.

It all comes down to how we tackle wicked problems. With curiosity, creativity, and collaboration, we can aim for transcendence. Otherwise, we risk collapse. The stakes couldn't be higher.

> *Don't look at things as they are, but as they could become.*

←#74 #73 →#76

#76 No Need to Choose

For companies, the choice often feels binary: chase short-term gains – exploit what you already know (noun-thinking) – or embrace long-term exploration (verb-thinking) with curiosity and experimentation at the forefront. But this perceived dilemma is a trap. The pressure to exploit can lead to long-term collapse if companies don't also invest in exploring new opportunities. Red companies risk collapse by focusing solely on the status quo, orange companies teeter on a plateau, and green companies – those that embrace curiosity – are set to transcend. Here's the thing: short-term success and long-term vision are not mutually exclusive. In fact, they can reinforce each other. This is where open perceptual loops and curiosity become essential. Open perceptual loops are feedback systems within a company that promote a continuous cycle of learning, adaptation, and improvement. By encouraging curiosity, companies not only prepare for future challenges but also maintain the flexibility to capitalise on immediate opportunities.

A business that values curiosity ensures that employees are always learning, experimenting, and thinking outside the box. This dynamic creates a workplace where short-term wins are achieved without sacrificing the long-term vision. In other words, you don't have to choose between today and tomorrow – you can win at both. Companies must recognise that cultivating a culture of curiosity doesn't detract from financial goals; it enhances them. Encouraging employees to ask questions, experiment, and develop new skills doesn't just keep them engaged – it's a pathway to innovation. This approach leads to continuous improvement, better products, and ultimately, higher profits.

This is why curiosity should be considered a Key Performance Indicator (KPI). Curiosity directly influences a company's ability to innovate, adapt, and thrive in today's fast-paced world. Traditional KPIs focus on tangible outcomes like financial performance, but in a business environment defined by constant change, we need broader measures of success. Let me break it down:

1. Innovation and Growth: Curiosity drives the discovery of new ideas and untapped markets, fuelling growth and differentiation.
2. Adaptability: In an ever-changing world, companies that prioritise learning and adaptability are better equipped to pivot when necessary. Curiosity powers that agility.
3. Employee Engagement: Curious employees are more invested in their work, leading to higher productivity and job satisfaction.
4. Customer Satisfaction: Companies that are curious about customer behaviour and preferences can create more tailored, meaningful experiences, which boosts loyalty.

By making curiosity a KPI, businesses ensure they're not just keeping up with the competition but leading it. Curiosity drives both the flexibility to address today's challenges and the foresight to seize tomorrow's opportunities. The only thing left? Making curiosity measurable. And I was getting closer.

←#75 #74 #73 →#77

#77 The Breakthrough

The classic S-curve is a model companies love – it shows how businesses grow from slow starts to explosive growth, then hit a saturation point where things slow down. The solution to stagnation? Stack the S-curves. Start a new growth cycle just as the old one begins to flatten out. This strategy, although familiar, misses one key point: the world is accelerating faster than your S-curves can stack.

Even with stacked S-curves, companies might only just keep up with external change but never truly lead the pack. That's where the Red Queen Principle comes in: companies must evolve continuously just to stay in the game. Leading companies, however, don't just evolve – they create reinforcing loops that drive exponential growth, turning them into industry leaders. These loops are born from innovative business models, groundbreaking technology, or a strong culture of constant learning and improvement. It's not enough to stack S-curves anymore; businesses must find ways to amplify growth, creating new possibilities where none existed before.

This is where curiosity becomes critical. By cultivating exploratory, empathic, and specific curiosity, companies foster an environment where continuous discovery leads to innovation. Here's how curiosity fits into the picture:
1. Exploratory curiosity propels employees to dive into the unknown, unafraid to take risks or embrace failure. It's the spark for new ideas.
2. Empathic curiosity sharpens understanding of customers and colleagues, ensuring that innovation is relevant and human-centred.

3. Specific curiosity allows employees to develop deep expertise, ensuring that new ideas are not just wild guesses but well-informed leaps forward.

To measure these types of curiosity, companies can track how often employees propose new projects, how willing they are to embrace feedback, and how deeply they dive into specialised areas of expertise. It was clear to me: curiosity had to be measured for businesses to thrive in this fast-paced world.

←#76#75#74#73 →Cycling Route Network 'Lost Curiosity'

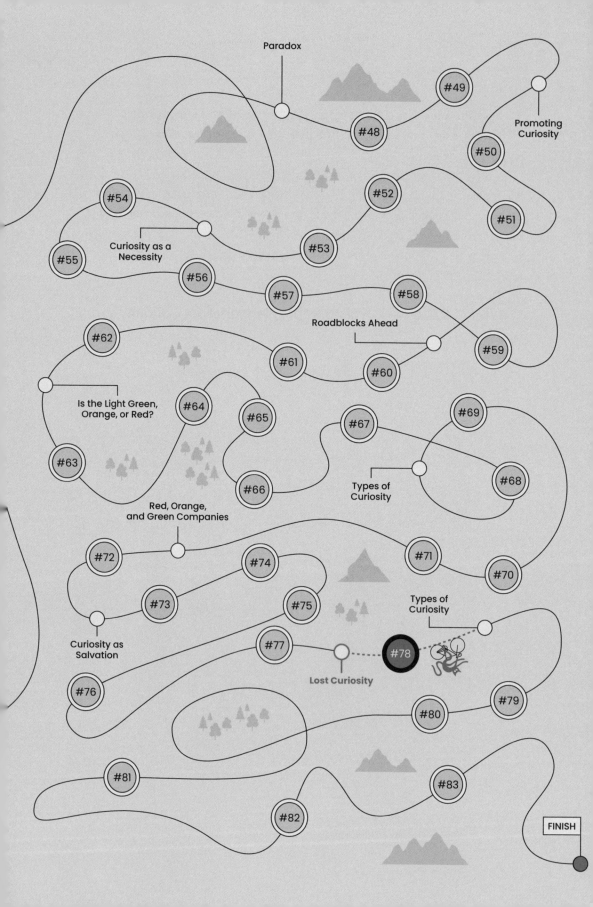

Cycling Route Network 'Lost Curiosity'

#78 Curiosity Lost

Just when you think you're nearing the finish line – final stretch of the book, a few thousand more words, a couple more cups of coffee – an email drops in. It's from a business leader, someone you've sparked with all your enthusiasm for curiosity. But instead of praise, it's a string of questions. And not just any questions, the kind that gets under your skin. Ones that make you pause mid-type, blink at the screen, and reconsider whether you've been clear enough, convincing enough. The subject line reads: "Why do children lose their innate curiosity?"

I was tempted to ignore it, hit 'mark as read' and carry on. But of course, I couldn't. I knew this person. If anyone could benefit from this book, it was this guy. So, I dove in.

"And," he added, "what can we, as a company, learn from that?"

I stared at the question for a while. Good question, actually. Frustratingly good. I started typing a response, something that hopefully would quench his curiosity – and mine in the process. Here's what I told him: Children are naturally curious, but as they grow older, this curiosity starts to fade. Here's why:

1. Comfort in Knowledge: As children learn more, they start feeling comfortable with what they already know. Instead of seeking out the new, they settle into familiar patterns.
2. Social and Educational Pressures: Kids learn that there are 'right' answers, and asking too many questions can make them feel foolish or slow.
3. Fear of Mistakes: Early on, mistakes are part of learning. But as kids get older, they're conditioned to see mistakes as failures rather than opportunities.

4. Information Overload: Kids, like adults, can get overwhelmed. Too much information and too many choices can make curiosity seem like a daunting, even futile, exercise.

So, what can companies learn from this? How do they keep curiosity alive in adults?
- Create a culture of learning: Just like kids need to be encouraged to explore, companies need to reward continuous learning and discovery.
- Value questioning: Make it clear that asking the right questions is often more valuable than having the right answers.
- Embrace mistakes: Let employees take risks and learn from their failures without fear of punishment.
- Manage information: Help employees navigate the flood of data and focus their curiosity on what matters most.
- Encourage diversity of thought: Just like kids thrive when they're allowed to explore different perspectives, employees should be encouraged to think differently, fostering innovation.

If companies don't prioritise curiosity – and measure it – all these good intentions will remain just that: intentions without action. That's when it hit me: curiosity had to become measurable if companies were to truly harness its power. And I was on the verge of figuring it out.

→Cycling Route Network 'Curiosity as a KPI'

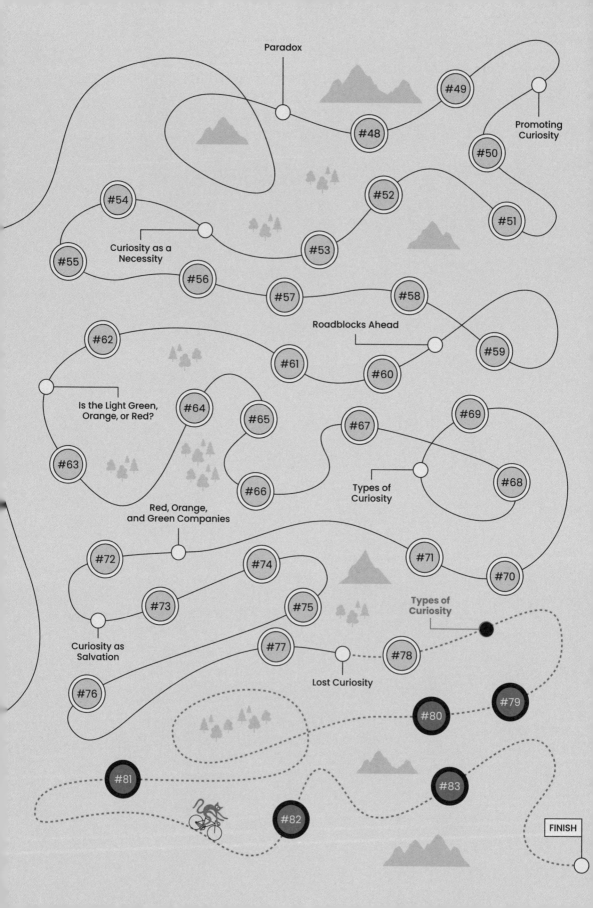

Cycling Route Network 'Curiosity as a KPI'

Where is that KPI?

#79 About a KPI, NPS, and NCS

How could I make curiosity measurable, turn it into a KPI, something tangible that organisations could actually use? Was this a far-fetched dream, or was it within reach? The challenge gnawed at me: how do you capture something as abstract as curiosity, bottle it up into a metric, and make it work for companies wrestling with the wicked problems on the horizon? I started tossing ideas around. What if we measured how many questions were asked in meetings? Or the number of new initiatives employees proposed? Maybe the diversity of ideas during brainstorming sessions? The willingness to take risks? All solid thoughts, but they were outcomes. They felt more like recommendations, a little too convoluted to serve as clean, direct measures. I needed something sharper, something simple.

And then, life threw me a curveball on a flight.

I found myself seated next to someone wearing the unmistakable badge of a consultant from a big-name firm. You know the type – sharp suit, sharp mind, sharp enough to cut through any nonsense. We got chatting, and naturally, I unloaded my struggle.

"Take the NPS score," I said, referencing the Net Promoter Score that businesses swear by. "It's genius in its simplicity. One question on a ten-point scale, and boom, it tells you everything about customer loyalty. That's why it's so successful – it distills something complex into something everyone can understand and use."

I leaned in a little, excited by my own words. "So, why can't I do the same for curiosity? Why does measuring curiosity have to be complicated? Couldn't I come up with something just as simple, just as effective – something that could go mainstream like the NPS?"

The consultant, clearly intrigued, nodded. "Simplicity is the key to adoption," he said, without missing a beat. "If you can strip curiosity down to its core and measure that, you'll have something people will actually use."

That conversation lingered with me. I couldn't shake it. It stuck in my mind like a pebble in your shoe – always there, always pushing you to keep thinking. By the time the flight was nearing its destination, I had barely slept, but I had something even better – an idea, a concept. A spark. I called it the Net Curiosity Score (NCS) – a tool designed to capture the richness and complexity of curiosity, boiled down into one simple, powerful metric. It felt... right. Here's what I came up with:

1. Single Core Question: Just like the NPS has one core question, so would the NCS. Something like: "*On a scale of 0 to 10, how likely are you to explore a new idea or unfamiliar subject in your work?*" It had to be clear and direct – no fuss, no ambiguity.
2. Scoring Mechanism:
    - Promoters (Score 9-10): These are your curiosity champions, the ones always out there exploring new ideas, actively seeking out knowledge.
    - Passives (Score 7-8): They're somewhat curious but don't always push themselves to dive deeper or consistently seek out new things.
    - Detractors (Score 0-6): These are the folks who show little interest in exploring beyond their comfort zone – if it's unfamiliar, they avoid it.
3. Calculating the Score: It was simple. The NCS would be calculated by subtracting the percentage of detractors from the percentage of promoters, giving a score between –100 (zero curiosity) and +100 (off-the-charts curiosity).

4. Additional Questions: To flesh out the insights, you could add follow-up questions, digging into how often employees exhibit curiosity-driven behaviour, their willingness to take risks, or how open they are to new ideas.

There it was. It was practical. It was simple. It was something organisations could grab hold of and run with. The NCS could sit next to the NPS as a pillar of measurement – just as customer loyalty is vital to business, so too is curiosity. A company's future depends on it. I knew I'd hit on something. Now, it was time to refine, smooth out the rough edges, and make the NCS a tool that companies couldn't live without. This was it. Curiosity as a KPI was no longer just an idea floating around – it was real. All that was left was to fine-tune it, to make it sing.

→ #80

#80 Towards a Net Curiosity Score

The idea kept growing, evolving in my mind. I realised that to truly capture the essence of curiosity within an organisation, I needed to flip that core question. Why? Because curiosity is a two-way street. It's not just about how curious employees are; it's about how much the company allows them to be curious. So, I thought: *"On a scale of 0 to 10, how easy is it for you to bring up new ideas or topics at work?"* This would give me the Organisational Curiosity Receptivity Score (OCRS), which would measure how open a company is to new ideas.

Together, the NCS and OCRS would provide a full picture: how curious employees are, and how supportive the company is of that curiosity. It would help identify any gap between what employees want to explore and what the company encourages. This could lead to targeted actions to boost both individual curiosity and company culture.

One evening, while sitting next to the CEO of an organisation during a dinner, I shared my growing idea with her. "It's all about measuring curiosity in your company," I said, watching her reaction carefully. "It may sound strange, but it's crucial for growth. Curiosity is the engine behind creativity, innovation, progress. It drives us to ask questions, to explore beyond the familiar, to find solutions to problems we haven't even identified yet. But how do we know if we are truly curious? How can we tell if our company culture supports that curiosity?"

She listened intently, nodding.

"This is where the NCS and OCRS come in," I continued. "They'll help measure both the curiosity of your employees and how open your company is to their ideas."

She smiled, intrigued. "Those two perspectives, and the gap between them – there's something there."

I pressed on. "I get that measuring curiosity might seem contradictory. We're used to measuring hard things like sales numbers and production times. But curiosity, though intangible, is just as critical. If we don't measure it, we can't improve it. The NCS and OCRS give us a way to quantify something as fundamental as curiosity. They'll help companies spot their strengths and uncover areas where they can improve. Right?"

Her marketing director and CFO joined the conversation, and we dove deeper. Soon, we were debating how curiosity could be measured in their customer base, especially after marketing campaigns. They were excited, and I was thrilled to see the concept take root in their minds. They even mentioned how curiosity could become a marketing tool. By the end of the evening, we had brainstormed a new idea: the Customer Curiosity Score (CCS), to measure how intrigued and interested consumers were in their products. But we were careful. We didn't want to fall into the trap of over-surveying customers. We agreed on the importance of respecting the customer's time, using indirect methods like social media engagement and website analytics to gauge curiosity without being too invasive. This conversation fuelled me. The NCS, OCRS, and CCS – these metrics were becoming real, each one adding a new layer to how curiosity could be understood and measured. It wasn't just about innovation anymore. It was about shaping the future of how companies operate, interact with their employees, and engage their customers.

←#79 →#81

Refinements

#81 Initial Refinements

As I neared the finish line on this book, the usual doubts crept in. I knew I had to make some refinements. One of the first things I reconsidered was the 10-point scale I had borrowed from the NPS. While the NPS was a popular tool for measuring customer loyalty, it had received its fair share of criticism – specifically, the cultural biases that different respondents brought to the 10-point scale. A 7 in one country might feel like a 9 in another.

I didn't want my NCS to suffer from the same issue. So, I decided to switch to a 7-point scale. It felt cleaner, less bound by tradition, and might provide a more accurate reflection of curiosity within an organisation. I also realised the terminology needed an overhaul. The NPS used the terms 'Promoters', 'Passives', and 'Detractors', but that language didn't sit right with curiosity. I wanted something that reflected action and potential. With that in mind, I redefined the classifications:
- Explorers (6-7): The trailblazers. Employees who are eager to explore new ideas and actively seek knowledge.
- Inquirers (4-5): The steady thinkers. They occasionally explore, but

not as consistently as Explorers.
- Observers (0-3): Those who prefer to stick with what they know, rarely venturing into new territory.

This felt better. 'Explorers' sounded positive, active, and forward-thinking – exactly the kind of people companies should want. 'Inquirers' had a nice neutral ring to it, while 'Observers' didn't carry the same negative baggage as 'Detractors'.

←#80 #79 → #82

#82 Additional Measurement

As I dug deeper into the mechanics of curiosity, I noticed something important: there's a difference between increasing receptivity and boosting curiosity within an organisation. Both are necessary, but they target different behaviours. Receptivity is about creating an environment where new ideas are welcomed, considered, and given a fair shot. It's about making sure employees know their ideas will be heard. To improve receptivity, companies could:
- Adopt an open-door policy for idea-sharing.
- Provide systems to evaluate and implement ideas fairly.
- Train leaders to actively listen and give constructive feedback.

But boosting curiosity was different. Boosting was about encouraging employees to be curious, to go out and seek new ideas. This was the proactive side of the equation. To boost curiosity, companies could:
- Offer incentives for innovative ideas.
- Run curiosity workshops and training sessions.
- Celebrate curiosity-driven successes to inspire others.

Both aspects – receptivity and boosting – needed to work in tandem to foster a truly curious organisation. They reinforced each other, creating an environment where curiosity could thrive. The more I thought about this, the more I realised another score was necessary. In addition to the OCRS, which measured how receptive a company was to new ideas, I needed a score that captured how much the company actively encouraged curiosity. So, I added the Organisational Curiosity Boosting Score (OCBS). This score would measure how much employees felt encouraged to explore new ideas.

Now, I had a framework that offered a 360-degree view of curiosity in an organisation: the NCS for individual curiosity, the OCRS for organisational receptivity, and the OCBS for how much companies encouraged curiosity. These three scores would paint a clear picture of how well curiosity was functioning at every level. It was holistic, actionable, and – most importantly – measureable. Finally, I was getting somewhere. Now it was time to take this idea and refine it into a tool that companies could actually use to drive real change.

←#81#80#79 →#83

#83 Three Dimensions

The breakthrough came when I realised that the Net Curiosity Score (NCS) shouldn't just be a singular measurement but a result of three distinct metrics working together. These metrics – PCS (Personal Curiosity Score), OCRS (Organisational Curiosity Receptivity Score), and OCBS (Organisational Curiosity Boosting Score) – formed the backbone of a multidimensional approach to curiosity within an organisation. Each one measured a different aspect of curiosity: personal, organisational receptivity, and how much the company actively encouraged it. The math was simple: take the three scores, add them up, and divide by three. Boom. That's your NCS.

But more than that, this approach would give a company real insights into how curiosity functioned across its different layers. By looking at the NCS Matrix, organisations could plot their curiosity health in a three-dimensional space, with PCS, OCRS, and OCBS acting as the three axes. Now curiosity wasn't just something abstract – it could be visualised, mapped, and, most importantly, acted upon.

Here's how I envisioned the matrix:
- X-axis (PCS): This represents individual curiosity – the extent to which employees are personally driven to explore, learn, and question.
- Y-axis (OCRS): The organisation's receptivity to curiosity. This tells us how open the company is to receiving and acting on new ideas.
- Z-axis (OCBS): Measures how much the company actively boosts curiosity – how much encouragement and motivation employees receive to keep exploring.

The NCS Matrix in Action

The magic of this matrix lies in the interaction between these three dimensions. By plotting scores for individuals, teams, or even entire organisations, you get a 3D snapshot of your curiosity landscape. For example:
- High PCS, high OCRS, low OCBS: This might indicate that employees are naturally curious, and the organisation is open to new ideas, but there's a lack of active encouragement or resources to nurture that curiosity. Employees are interested, but they aren't getting the fuel they need.
- High PCS, high OCBS, low OCRS: This shows a company that encourages curiosity and has employees who are eager to explore but lacks the necessary structures and processes to turn those ideas into action. It's like asking for great ideas and then filing them away in a drawer.
- Low PCS, high OCRS, high OCBS: Here, the organisation is set up perfectly to receive and boost curiosity, but the individuals within the team aren't stepping up. This might point to a need for personal development or new motivation strategies.

Where to Focus?

As I dug deeper, it became clear that each quadrant of the NCS Ma-

trix would offer actionable insights for improvement. A company could focus on:
- Boosting Personal Curiosity (PCS): Encouraging employees to take risks, ask questions, and stay curious. This could involve training, new challenges, or creating a culture where learning is rewarded.
- Improving Organisational Receptivity (OCRS): Ensuring that the company is set up to not only listen to but also act on new ideas. This might involve breaking down hierarchies, fostering better communication channels, or ensuring leaders are open to feedback.
- Supercharging Curiosity Boosting (OCBS): Actively pushing curiosity within the organisation. This is where the company says, "We want more curiosity, and we're going to actively invest in it." That could mean providing resources, offering incentives, or launching innovation labs.

Simplifying the Complexity

As much as I loved the idea of diving deep into every nuance of curiosity, I knew that simplicity was the key to making the NCS work. The challenge was to ensure that it didn't become so complicated that it was unusable. So I kept refining:

1. PCS: This could be measured on an individual, team, or organisation-wide level. It's the most flexible of the three.
2. OCRS and OCBS: These are broader scores, best measured at the team or organisational level. They show how the environment supports curiosity.
3. High, Transition, Low: Just like with NPS, benchmarks are crucial. For now, I've found that scores above 50 are strong, and anything below zero is a warning sign. Scores between 0 and 50? Those are 'transition' scores – areas where curiosity is either growing or diminishing.
4. The 8-Box Model: A full 3D matrix could get messy. With three axes and multiple variables, you end up with 27 possible 'boxes' or scenarios, which feels overwhelming. So I reduced it to eight by focusing on high or low scores on each axis. When comparing teams or individuals, anything above the average score is high, and

anything below is low. Without formal benchmarks, I suggest that for the company as a whole, <25 is low and >25 is high.

Interpreting the Matrix

Once plotted, the NCS Matrix becomes a powerful tool for leaders. You can see exactly where teams or individuals are excelling and where improvement is needed.

- High on all three axes (PCS, OCRS, OCBS)? That's a team firing on all curiosity cylinders – curious employees who are supported and actively encouraged by their company. This is where innovation thrives.
- Low on all three? That's a red flag. These teams are in danger of stagnation, with neither the individuals nor the organisation pushing curiosity forward. This is where companies start to fall behind.

By regularly measuring and adjusting based on the NCS, companies could avoid complacency and create environments that thrive on curiosity. It would help shape interventions, adjust processes, and, ultimately, ensure that curiosity remained a driving force behind progress and innovation.

From Theory to Practice

As I tinkered with the matrix, I kept one thing in mind: this has to be practical. Filling in and interpreting the matrix had to be simple, accessible, and – most importantly – useful. The whole point was to make curiosity actionable. And this 3D model – the **NCS Matrix** – would be the key to that. Not only could companies visualise their curiosity health, but they could also take specific actions to improve it.

Playbook

Your Key to Innovation

In today's rapidly changing business world, innovation is no longer a luxury – it's a necessity. Companies that want to stay ahead must continually find new ways to innovate and maintain their competitive edge. This is where the NCS Matrix comes in, a methodology that helps businesses uncover and optimise their hidden innovation potential.

What is the NCS?

The NCS (Net Curiosity Score) is the average of three measurements: Personal Curiosity Score (PCS), Organisational Curiosity Receptivity Score (OCRS), and Organisational Curiosity Boosting Score (OCBS).

What is the NCS Matrix?

The NCS Matrix is a simple yet powerful tool that measures a core question on a 7-point scale across three axes:
1. Personal Curiosity (PCS): How curious are your employees?
2. Organisational Curiosity Receptivity (OCRS): How open is your organisation to new ideas?
3. Organisational Curiosity Boosting (OCBS): To what extent does your company stimulate curiosity?

Why Should Your Company Use the NCS Matrix?

- Simplicity and Efficiency: The NCS Matrix is quick and easy to implement, providing insights into your organisation without sig-

nificant investment of time or resources.
- Measurable Innovation: The NCS Matrix offers a concrete KPI for innovation, allowing you to track progress and make targeted improvements.
- Enhanced Collaboration: By focusing on curiosity, the NCS Matrix promotes collaboration and knowledge sharing across departments.
- Flexibility: Adapting to market changes becomes easier when your team learns to think innovatively and pivot quickly.
- Optimal Resource Use: The NCS Matrix helps in efficiently deploying your human capital by aligning the right people with the right projects.

How Does It Work?

Using the NCS Matrix is surprisingly straightforward. Start with a core question that gauges curiosity within your organisation. Then, use the 7-point scale to measure how your organisation scores on the three axes of the matrix. These scores provide immediate insight into where your organisation stands and where there's room for improvement.

1. **The Scale**
   Scores are measured on a scale of 0 to 7.
   0-3: Low
   4-5: Average
   6-7: High

2. **Methodology**
   For larger groups, subtract the percentage of low scores (0-3) from the percentage of high scores (6-7), ignoring the average scores (4-5). For smaller teams (<10), simply review the scores without applying this calculation.

3. **High/Transition/Low**
   Since there are no established benchmarks yet, and because, simi-

lar to the NPS, what constitutes 'good', 'exceptional', 'average', and 'low' scores can vary, I suggest the following:
High: Scores over 50
Transition: Scores between 0 and 50
Low: Scores below 0

4. 8-Box
To simplify analysis in the three-dimensional space, where plotting on all three axes would result in a complex tangle of 27 areas or boxes, reduce this to 8 boxes by focusing only on high or low on each axis. Consider:
Low: Scores <25
High: Scores >25

Step-by-Step Guide

1. **Measure the PCS (Personal Curiosity Score)**

Core Question 01:
"On a scale of 0 to 7, how likely are you to explore a new idea or an unfamiliar topic in your work?"

Scoring Mechanism:
- **Explorers (6-7):** Employees who are very inclined to explore new ideas and actively seek knowledge.
- **Inquirers (4-5):** Employees who show average curiosity and occasionally explore new areas.
- **Observers (0-3):** Employees who are less active in their curiosity and rarely take the initiative to investigate new ideas.

Score Calculation:
Calculate the PCS by subtracting the percentage of observers from the percentage of explorers, yielding a score between –100 (no curiosity) and +100 (extreme curiosity).

Additional Questions:
For deeper insights, additional questions can be asked about the frequency of curious behaviour, the diversity of topics explored, and the willingness to take risks.

2. **Measure the OCRS (Organisational Curiosity Receptivity Score)**

Core Question 02:
"On a scale of 0 to 7, how easy is it for you to bring up new ideas or topics at work?"

Scoring Mechanism:
- **Active Supporter (6-7):** Companies with active green and orange boxes, striving to keep the red box empty.
- **Flexible Integrator (4-5):** Companies developing green and orange boxes and attempting to empty the red box.
- **Reserved Responder (0-3):** Companies with no green or orange boxes.

Score Calculation:
Calculate the OCRS by subtracting the percentage of reserved responders from the percentage of active supporters, yielding a score between −100 (no receptivity) and +100 (extreme receptivity).

3. Measure the OCBS (Organisational Curiosity Boosting Score)

Core Question 03:
"On a scale of 0 to 7, how much does the company motivate you to bring up new ideas or topics at work?"

Scoring Mechanism:
- **Curiosity Champion (6-7):** Companies that actively encourage employees to be curious.
- **Progressive Enhancer (4-5):** Companies that encourage employees

to be curious.
- **Passive Observer (0-3):** Companies that do not encourage curiosity among employees.

Score Calculation:
Calculate the OCBS by subtracting the percentage of passive observers from the percentage of curiosity champions, yielding a score between −100 (no boosting) and +100 (extreme boosting).

4. Calculate the NCS: (PCS + OCRS + OCBS) / 3
5. Plot the Results as High/Low

Plot the measured results on the three axes. Since the PCS is measured individually, this axis can be filled in for individuals, departments, or the entire company. I recommend not approaching the two company-related axes individually but rather by department or for the whole company.

Plot the result as High/Transition/Low:
High: >50
Transition: 0-50
Low: <0

6. **Check the box**

In the three-dimensional model with the Net Curiosity Score (NCS), Organisational Curiosity Receptivity Score (OCRS), and Organisational Curiosity Boosting Score (OCBS) as axes, we can identify the following eight zones:

1. Curiosity Champions (High PCS, High OCRS, High OCBS): Employees are very curious, and the organisation actively supports and stimulates this, resulting in a culture of innovation and growth.
    - For the Employee: A rich environment for personal and professional development.

- For the Company: A source of constant innovation and competitive advantage.
- Improvement: Continue investing in developing curiosity and creating opportunities for exploration.

2. Curiosity Pioneers (High PCS, High OCRS, Low OCBS): Employees are curious, and the organisation is receptive, but there is a lack of stimulation.
    - For the Employee: Opportunity to take a leading role in innovation.
    - For the Company: Potential for growth that is not fully realised.
    - Improvement: Implement programs that reward and stimulate curiosity.

3. Curiosity Learners (Low PCS, High OCRS, High OCBS): Employees are less curious but are encouraged to develop this trait.
    - For the Employee: Opportunities for growth through support and stimulation.
    - For the Company: Talent development that can lead to future innovation.
    - Improvement: Personal development plans aimed at increasing curiosity.

4. Curiosity Seekers (High PCS, Low OCRS, High OCBS): Employees are curious but do not feel fully supported by the organisation.
    - For the Employee: Frustration due to a lack of organisational support.
    - For the Company: Missed opportunities due to not recognising individual contributions.
    - Improvement: Increase the organisation's receptivity to new ideas.

5. Curiosity Contributors (Low PCS, Low OCRS, High OCBS): There is an attempt to stimulate curiosity, but both employees and the organisation are passive.

- For the Employee: Little personal drive to explore and innovate.
- For the Company: A culture not conducive to curiosity.
- Improvement: Stimulate culture change and personal growth.

6. Curiosity Innovators (High PCS, High OCRS, Low OCBS): Employees are curious, and the organisation is receptive, but there is little stimulation.
    - For the Employee: Potential to innovate is not fully realised.
    - For the Company: Lack of resources to support curiosity.
    - Improvement: Provide more resources and opportunities to explore curiosity.

7. Curiosity Observers (Low PCS, High OCRS, Low OCBS): Employees are not very curious, but the organisation is open to ideas.
    - For the Employee: Limited contribution to innovation.
    - For the Company: Untapped potential due to a lack of employee motivation.
    - Improvement: Training and motivation programs to stimulate curiosity.

8. Curiosity Dormants (Low PCS, Low OCRS, Low OCBS): Both employees and the organisation show little curiosity.
    - For the Employee: Lack of stimulus to grow or innovate.
    - For the Company: Stagnation and lack of competitive advantage.
    - Improvement: Develop a comprehensive strategy to create a culture of curiosity.

Each zone presents unique challenges and opportunities for both employees and the company. By focusing on the characteristics of each zone, organisations can develop targeted strategies to cultivate and leverage curiosity as a driving force for innovation and growth.

Curiosity for Advanced Practitioners

Whether you have navigated this playbook by following the chapter paths or simply read from start to finish, you might now be thinking: these core questions are very generic, but what about the three types of curiosity we discussed, all of which are important? You know:

1. **Explorative Curiosity:** The drive to explore and acquire new knowledge. It encourages employees to think outside the box and seek unconventional solutions.
2. **Empathic Curiosity:** The ability to empathise with customers and colleagues. This leads to a better understanding of their needs and desires, crucial for creating valuable products and services.
3. **Specific Curiosity:** The focus on deeply understanding specific subjects. This fosters expertise and detailed insights that can lead to innovation within a field.

The core questions I've proposed are indeed generic and primarily align with explorative curiosity. This is intentional. Like the NPS, I aim to keep the measurement of curiosity simple and accessible.

For companies looking to dive deeply into exploring curiosity or wanting to measure how they perform in the three areas or those focusing on a particular type of curiosity for specific reasons, different core questions could be used. These questions could be plotted on the same three axes to see how curious employees are, how receptive the organisation is to that specific curiosity, and how much employees are encouraged to pursue that particular curiosity.

For example, companies wanting to empty their red box of missed opportunities and needing rapid reactive innovation might benefit more from fostering specific curiosity first. Companies needing better knowledge and understanding of their customers might initially focus more on empathic curiosity and then measure and cultivate it.

However, I hope it's clear after reading this book that these are temporary measures and that, in the long run, companies are better served by either asking the generic question or asking three types of core questions that simultaneously monitor all three types of curiosity. Consider it 'advanced curiosity'. Such companies know how to fill the green box, keep the orange box alive, and quickly and alertly address the few matters that might end up in the red box.

What Are the Three Core Questions?

Generic/Explorative

PCS: "On a scale of 0 to 7, how likely are you to explore a new idea or an unfamiliar topic in your work?"
Receptive Score: "On a scale of 0 to 7, how easy is it for you to bring up new ideas or topics at work?"
Boosting Score: "On a scale of 0 to 7, how much does the company motivate you to bring up new ideas or topics at work?"

Empathic

PCS: "On a scale of 0 to 7, how likely are you to explore a new idea or better understand customers?"
Receptive Score: "On a scale of 0 to 7, how easy is it for you to bring up new ideas or better understand customers at work?"
-Boosting Score: "On a scale of 0 to 7, how much does the company motivate you to bring up new ideas or better understand customers at work?"

Specific

PCS: "On a scale of 0 to 7, how likely are you to explore a new idea or gain better knowledge in your work-related expertise field?"
Receptive Score: "On a scale of 0 to 7, how easy is it for you to bring

up new ideas or gain better knowledge in your work-related expertise field at work?"

Boosting Score: "On a scale of 0 to 7, how much does the company motivate you to bring up new ideas or gain better knowledge in your work-related expertise field at work?"

Beyond the Innovation Department: Building a Culture Where Curiosity Can Thrive

'The next big breakthrough isn't hiding in an innovation lab; it's waiting in the minds of people who feel safe enough to dream out loud every day.'

When I watch my granddaughters lost in play, it's like stepping into a parallel universe. They don't just play with dolls; they create entire worlds. In their eyes, a doll isn't a doll—it's a queen, a scientist, an astronaut on a secret mission. There are no rules, no limits, no self-doubt. They shape reality as they please, letting their imaginations run free. Watching them, I can't help but wonder: why does that magic fade as we grow up? Why do we stop feeling safe enough to let our ideas roam as wildly?

In companies, we've built entire structures to 'encourage innovation.' There are in-house startups, shiny innovation departments, creative spaces with bean bags and whiteboards, and slogans about 'thinking outside the box.' But let's be honest—how many of these initiatives lead to breakthroughs that genuinely shake up traditional industries? For all the resources and talk, most of the results are... safe. Incremental improvements, tweaks to existing products, a fresh design maybe. But true breakthroughs? Transformations that redefine an industry or invent something new altogether? They're as rare as ever.

Why is that? Why, despite all these efforts to foster creativity, are we still stuck in the old ways?

Playing It Safe in the Innovation Sandbox

Here's the problem: these 'innovation labs' and 'in-house startups' are often just another layer of control. They're neatly fenced-off spaces where creativity is allowed to play, but only within boundaries. People are invited to come up with 'big ideas'—but not too big, not too risky, and definitely nothing that threatens the status quo. It's like giving children a sandbox and telling them to build a castle, but only out of the sand that's already there. No bringing in new materials, no digging outside the lines.

Real breakthroughs require a different mindset. They need people who feel safe enough to take genuine risks, to question everything, and to challenge sacred cows. But traditional industries, by nature, are resistant to this kind of disruption. They've built themselves on decades, sometimes centuries, of rules, structures, and established norms. Allowing real, boundary-pushing innovation means inviting chaos—and that's a terrifying prospect for most companies.

Innovation Isn't Just for the 'Innovation Department'

We talk about innovation as if it's a department's job. But here's the truth: innovation is everyone's job. The most revolutionary ideas rarely come from a designated team of 'creatives.' They come from people who see things differently because they're inside the day-to-day, noticing inefficiencies, spotting customer pain points, and understanding where things don't quite work. Yet, we isolate innovation, assigning it to specific people, while the rest of the company is expected to 'keep things running.'

The irony? The people closest to the actual work, the ones who live and breathe it every day, are often the best equipped to imagine a different way of doing things. But in most companies, they don't feel safe to suggest anything radical. They stick to what's expected, afraid of rocking the boat, of seeming impractical or unrealistic. They have ideas—wild, ambitious, game-changing ideas—but they don't dare to share them.

Why Adults Fear the Imagination of a Child

There's a reason we're comfortable with children playing imaginary games but uneasy with adults who think too imaginatively. Children's fantasies are harmless; they're 'just playing.' But adults with big imaginations? They're seen as a threat, as people who might challenge the rules we've carefully constructed. They could propose ideas that don't fit into the quarterly earnings model or KPIs. And so, companies stifle them, unknowingly clipping the wings of the very people who might lead them to the next big thing.

Yet, every meaningful advancement, every piece of progress, owes itself to someone's bold imagination—someone who dared to wonder, 'What if...?' We need the audacity of curiosity, the bravery to dream like children. Because that's where true innovation lives, in the minds of people unafraid to envision a world that doesn't yet exist.

The Real Challenge: Making Curiosity Safe

If companies want real breakthroughs, they need to stop fencing off innovation. They need to build a culture where every employee, in every role, feels safe enough to share wild ideas. Not just the 'creatives' in the innovation department, but the accountant, the warehouse manager, the customer service rep. They all bring unique perspectives, and they all have ideas. The challenge is creating an environment where they feel safe to voice them, where they're not laughed at or ignored but encouraged to dream out loud.

This isn't easy. It requires leaders who are willing to let go of control, who value exploration as much as execution, and who understand that real progress is unpredictable. It means celebrating questions, not just answers, and fostering a culture that values imagination over immediate results.

The Risk of Staying Safe

The cost of playing it safe is high. Companies that fail to embrace real curiosity risk becoming irrelevant. They get stuck in the comfort of what's worked before, never daring to step into the unknown. They make small improvements while competitors or entirely new industries redefine the market. The truth is, the next big breakthrough won't come from the comfort zone. It'll come from the edges, from people willing to push boundaries and explore what's possible.

The Call to Dream, Every Day

So, as I watch my granddaughters play, I see a reminder of what's possible when imagination is unbound. Their play isn't just a game; it's a lesson in daring to dream, to create worlds without limitations. Imagine if every company encouraged that level of creativity in the workplace—not as a special event or a designated role, but as a daily practice. Imagine if every employee felt empowered to bring their wildest ideas to the table.

Because real innovation isn't about a few 'creative types' in a corner office. It's about creating a culture where everyone feels safe to imagine, where every 'What if…?' is valued, and where the next breakthrough can come from anyone, anywhere. That's the kind of environment that leads to true transformation. And that's the kind of world we need to build—one where imagination, like that of a child, is seen as a strength, not a threat.

Practical Insights: Creating 'Playtime' for Innovation in Your Business

We've explored how curiosity drives innovation, creativity, growth, customer-centricity, and a more enjoyable workplace. Now, let's talk about 'playtime'.

Ever watched kids at play? They're in a different world. A world beyond past, present, and future. I call it 'playtime' – a bubble where they can explore without the weight of reality. In that bubble, they process the world, practice life, and do it all while pouring 'pretend tea' to grandpa Peter (that's me). They've invited me into their Wonderland.

What does this have to do with business?

Wonderland in business – that's where I'm going. Do companies have their own 'playtime'? A space where people can ideate freely without the pressure of immediate results? Or are we stuck in a world where every sip of 'pretend tea' is met with, "What's the ROI on that?"

Many companies have their version of 'Wonderland': bean bags, ping-pong tables, scribbled windows, and quirky office furniture. But is there real playtime? Or does the pressure to deliver choke creativity before it even starts? No wonder companies hit a standstill – they've forgotten to create real playtime.

How to Create "Playtime" in Your Company

Here's how you bring back playtime. Practical, straightforward, and proven. Sometimes by design, other times by happy accident.

1. Avoid Getting Too Comfortable
   Challenge yourself and your team constantly. If you're too cosy in a role, it's time to switch gears. Curiosity dies in comfort zones. Stay curious, stay sharp.
2. Always Question the Status Quo
   Are you really understanding your customers? Are you truly delivering exceptional experiences? Innovation begins with questioning the status quo – every single day.
3. Seek External Help
   If you lack the expertise, bring it in. Expertise doesn't always need to be industry-specific. Find partners who can cross-pollinate new ideas from other sectors.

4. Cultivate a Curious Culture
   Lead by example. Show curiosity, encourage it, reward it. Run campaigns around curiosity – set timeframes, challenge your team, find solutions.
5. Value Questions Over Answers
   Foster a culture where questions are prized. Curiosity fuels creativity, and creativity drives business success. Encourage employees to ask 'why', 'how', and 'what if'.

Overcoming Barriers to Curiosity

Even the best intentions can get bogged down. There are barriers – here's how to knock them down.

- Fear of Risk and Inefficiency
  Curiosity feels like chaos to the efficiency-obsessed. But creative thinking needs space to be inefficient first. That's where breakthroughs happen.
- Lack of Time
  Tight deadlines kill curiosity. If your employees don't have time to think, they won't. You have to make time for learning and exploration.
- Fixed Mindset
  When people think abilities are static, curiosity stalls. Challenge this mindset. Growth and innovation happen when we stretch beyond what we know.
- Organisational Norms
  If efficiency and output rule, curiosity withers. Curiosity thrives where experimentation is celebrated, not feared.
- No Psychological Safety
  If your employees fear judgment or failure, they won't ask 'why' or 'how'. Foster a safe space where exploring ideas – even the wild ones – gets applause, not criticism.
- Short-Term Focus
  Curiosity doesn't always yield instant results. But long-term innovation depends on it. Don't let short-term goals snuff out curiosity.
- Lack of Learning Support
  When companies don't invest in development, curiosity dries up. If

there's no room for growth, why be curious?
- No Leadership Role Models
  If leaders don't model curiosity, no one else will follow. Curiosity starts at the top – lead by example.

Cultivating Curiosity: Practical Tips
Now for the fun part – making it happen.
- Ask More Questions
  Challenge yourself and your team to ask more questions. Curiosity starts by noticing what you don't know.
- Expand Your Knowledge
  Read widely, listen to podcasts, attend webinars. Curiosity grows with exposure to different perspectives and knowledge.
- Embrace Uncertainty
  Be comfortable with not knowing. Embrace the ambiguity – it's where discovery lives.
- Reflect on Learning
  Take time to think about what you've learned. Curiosity isn't just about gathering facts; it's about understanding how you learn and grow.
- Practice Self-Development
  Push yourself to learn new skills, challenge your assumptions, and stay curious.
- Create Learning Journeys
  Some organisations create structured 'learning journeys' – deliberate programs designed to expand curiosity. It's a great way to keep the curiosity engine running.

The Power of Curiosity in Organisations
Curiosity isn't just a fluffy 'nice-to-have'. It's a business essential. Here's why:
1. Engagement and Meaning
   Curious employees are engaged. They find meaning in their work and push boundaries. Curiosity makes work fulfilling.
2. Performance

Curious employees perform better. Their drive to learn fuels their success, leading to higher satisfaction and better results.
3. Innovation
A culture of curiosity is a culture of innovation. Curious employees bring fresh ideas, creativity, and bold thinking.
4. Adaptability
In today's world, adaptability is critical. Curious employees embrace change and are better equipped to evolve with it.
5. Personal Growth
Curiosity fuels personal and professional growth, giving employees a greater sense of career satisfaction.
6. Positive Work Environment
Curiosity makes work dynamic. It creates a positive environment where learning, exploration, and teamwork thrive.
7. Social Connections
Curious employees build better relationships. Their desire to understand their colleagues creates a collaborative, supportive work culture.

Fostering curiosity isn't just about keeping people happy – it's about driving better outcomes. It leads to innovation, engagement, and a thriving business.

Afterword

Innovation at Sea

Why the Boardroom Keeps Passing the Buck

Here's a devastating fact: the same scenario plays out in boardrooms time after time, and we've somehow accepted it as *normal*. It's become a formula, like we're trapped in a corporate version of *Groundhog Day*. The room falls silent. Someone dares to bring up a new idea—half-formed, vulnerable, *risky*. And instead of embracing it, instead of nurturing that spark, what do we do? We pass the buck. We appoint another manager with a shiny new title. We create a new department to do what the C-suite should be doing themselves. Problem solved, right? No, not at all.

Instead of owning responsibility, we layer it. We get a Chief Digital Officer with a Digital Department, as if 'going digital' were a thing you could silo off in a corner. We hire a Social Media Manager because clearly, someone else needs to handle all that messy interaction with customers.

And here's the real devastating fact: an Innovation Manager and an Innovation Department. I mean, if *that* doesn't scream avoidance, what does?

You know the phrase: 'We're a tanker, so we need speedboats.' What the f—? *You're* responsible for that tanker. It's not someone else's job to steer. Innovation shouldn't be some side hustle you outsource to a bunch of speedboats while you sit in the captain's chair pretending the iceberg isn't there. The C-suite should be driving innovation, not delegating it.

The Beatles Didn't Need an Innovation Department

Now, let's contrast this corporate dysfunction with The Beatles. I've been diving into those iconic clips again—you know the ones. Picture it: George, Paul, or John walks in with an idea that's barely more than a sketch. Maybe some scribbled lyrics, maybe a half-strummed chord progression. You can almost see the thought bubble over their heads: *'Is this anything? Or is it complete garbage?'*

But what happens next is pure magic. The others don't mock it, don't shut it down with questions about ROI. Instead, they gather around the idea. Paul adds a riff. John nods and throws in a harmony. Ringo starts tapping out a beat. Before you know it, that scrappy little idea is morphing into something that could—and will—be legendary. Beatles magic. It's collaboration at its rawest and most vulnerable, the kind of magic that happens when everyone feels safe enough to show up with something unfinished.

Now, let's drag that scenario into the typical boardroom:
Exec #1: 'I've got this idea…'
Exec #2: 'Did you run it by Finance? Legal? Marketing? What's the projected ROI? Have you forecasted the Q4 impact?'
Exec #1: '…Never mind.'

That's the problem. Instead of fostering innovation, we kill it with red tape and spreadsheets. In the C-suite, vulnerability is like kryptonite. No one wants to show up with an idea that's not fully formed. That's why we keep appointing Innovation Managers to do the creative heavy lifting.

But let's be real: The Beatles didn't need an Innovation Manager. They didn't silo off creativity. They just needed a room, some instruments, and each other. That's the difference. Real innovation isn't outsourced—it's born in the messy, chaotic process of raw ideas colliding and evolving. And that, my friends, is what's missing in boardrooms today.

Corporate Fear of Vulnerability: Where Creativity Goes to Die

So why do boardrooms fail where The Beatles thrived? One word: fear. The C-suite is terrified of being vulnerable. If you're an executive, you're expected to have it all figured out, right? No half-baked ideas. No stumbling through rough drafts. In the corporate world, bringing an unfinished idea into the room is like walking into *Shark Tank*—except the sharks are your colleagues, and you're the chum.

Most execs would rather dive headfirst into a vat of spreadsheets than walk into a meeting with something unpolished. So, what do they do? They create departments to keep innovation at a safe distance. It's like they're saying, 'Sure, we love innovation, just keep it over there where it can't mess up my PowerPoint.'

'Vulnerability is not winning or losing; it's having the courage to show up when you can't control the outcome', says Brené Brown in her book *Dare to Lead*. And she's right. But in most boardrooms, courage takes a backseat to safety. And that's where innovation dies—*before* it even has a chance to breathe.

'You Never Give Me Your Money'—The Death of Safe Spaces in Business

Remember *Abbey Road*? The masterpiece where The Beatles somehow turned a collection of song fragments into one seamless suite? Each idea, no matter how small or incomplete, was given its moment to shine before handing the baton to the next. It's collaboration at its finest. They created a safe space for ideas to grow, stumble, and evolve. Now, think about your last corporate meeting. Did anyone walk in with a 'song snippet' and say, 'Hey, this is incomplete, but it could be something'? Or did you spend hours poring over spreadsheets and P&Ls, pretending everything was neat and tidy?

The problem is we don't give ideas room to grow. We strangle them in the cradle with questions like, 'What's the business case for that?'

In his book *Creativity, Inc.*, Pixar's Ed Catmull talks about how messy creativity is—how the early versions of every Pixar film were *terrible*. But Pixar thrived because they created a culture where early ideas could be awful, and no one got laughed out of the room. Their magic lay in the safe space they created for ideas to be bad before they could get good.

Let It Be Vulnerable: Why the C-Suite Needs to Take Responsibility

As Paul McCartney said, '*Let it be.*' Let ideas be raw, unfinished, vulnerable. Let them walk into the room with their shirt on inside out. Because only in spaces where people feel safe enough to be vulnerable will true innovation happen.

The Beatles didn't need to outsource creativity. They *owned* it. They took the responsibility to create, collaborate, and be vulnerable with each other. That's exactly what the C-suite needs to do. Innovation isn't something you can delegate. It's your job to create the environment where ideas can stumble, grow, and—eventually—succeed. So stop outsourcing innovation to a department. Stop passing the buck. Own it. Create a boardroom that feels more like a Beatles studio and less like a corporate battlefield. Because without that space for play, for vulnerability, for creativity, your company will stay stuck in the real tense—safely stagnant while the world moves on.

The Sgt. Pepper Lesson—No Surveys, Just Vision

When The Beatles created *Sgt. Pepper's Lonely Hearts Club Band*, they didn't commission expensive surveys or run focus groups to figure out if there was a market for it. They didn't sit around analyzing spreadsheets to determine whether their audience wanted a psychedelic concept album. They didn't try to *predict* what would sell. Instead, they trusted their instincts, pushed boundaries, and let their creativity take the lead.

Imagine the conversation if *Sgt. Pepper* had been born in today's corporate world: Exec #1: 'We're thinking of a concept album, something experimental with a fictional band and wild, colorful sounds.' Exec #2: 'Hmm, have we run the numbers on that? What's the target demographic? Can we get some focus group feedback? We need projections before we invest.' And just like that, *Sgt. Pepper* would've been dead before it even started. But The Beatles weren't interested in market validation. They didn't need a green light from some third-party consultant to tell them whether their creativity had value. They just *created*. They experimented. They played. And the result? One of the greatest, most influential albums in history.

Here's the takeaway: *Sgt. Pepper* is a masterpiece because it wasn't driven by market demand or data analysis. It was driven by vision. The Beatles trusted their instincts and believed in their ability to create something revolutionary. They weren't chasing a market; they were leading it. Now, think about your last big corporate project. How much time did you spend running surveys, testing markets, and seeking validation before you even put pen to paper? And how much of that time could've been spent simply *creating* something bold, something new, something no focus group could ever predict?

True innovation doesn't come from market validation. It comes from vision. If The Beatles had relied on surveys, we'd have missed out on one of the greatest albums of all time. The question isn't *what does the market want?* The question is, *what do you want to create that will change the market?*

Final Thought: Innovation Needs Courage

'Courage is resistance to fear, mastery of fear—not absence of fear.' – Mark Twain

And that's the truth. The boardroom needs courage—your courage. It's time to stop passing the buck and start creating a space where innovation isn't something you fear, but something you own.

Curiosity is the key to staying competitive, innovative, and adaptable. It's time to create a space where curiosity, learning, and creativity thrive. Welcome to your company's 'Wonderland'.

Diversity, Inclusion, Psychological Safety, and Curiosity

Once upon a time, my wife pointed out something I hadn't noticed, and it triggered a complete rethinking of our business model. But the most eye-opening moment? That came courtesy of my daughter. Picture this: a trip to the Netherlands to "show her what Dad does". She's about eight, full of opinions (as she always has been). I decided to take her to the design department – because hey, what kid doesn't love colours and textiles, right?

After ten minutes, she looks at me, unimpressed, and says, "This is boring." So I introduce her to Jan, our veteran product developer. Jan beams and pulls out what he calls "a real novelty" – a carpet designed for the youth. He shows it off like it's the next iPhone. My daughter? Not impressed. She says it looks like "old people carpet". Ouch. Jan, trying to win her over, asks, "Wouldn't you want this in your room?" Her answer? "Nope. It's ugly." And when he insists colours have numbers – "Ah, colour 34!" – she responds with pure childlike wisdom: "That's stupid. A colour isn't a number."

Jan didn't love this brutal honesty, but she was right. The carpet was boring, and the colours were dull. But the lesson wasn't just about taste. My daughter, the outsider, saw something the 'experts' missed, and that perspective opened a whole new conversation.

Later that night, my daughters handed me a paper filled with vibrant colours, each carefully labelled with 'fun' names – Barbie Pink, Race-car Red. They wrote, "Tell Jan these are the colours kids want in their rooms. Not old people colours. And no, colours don't have numbers." It was cute, and honestly, kind of brilliant.

The next day, I went to Jan, who didn't want to hear it. "I've been doing this for 35 years," he said, "I'm not letting a child tell me how to do my job." I let it drop. Or so I thought.

A week later, Jan bursts into my office with samples of pink, blue, orange, and the whole rainbow. "I showed these to my granddaughter," he said, "and she loved them. We'll call it 'Touché'. Our slogan? 'There's no excuse for being boring.'" He even labelled the colours with fun names, just like my daughters suggested. The rest is history – Touché became a hit, blowing up the beige and brown world of carpets, and kids everywhere were soon living in a Barbie Pink dream world.

What's the point? It's all about psychological safety – my daughter felt safe enough to share her truth (even if it was a little blunt), and Jan, after some reflection, found a way to embrace it.

Embracing Curiosity, Diversity, and Inclusion

Curiosity is a superpower. It drives innovation, fuels creativity, and – here's the kicker – it's magnified by diversity and inclusion. Diverse teams bring different lenses to the table, which leads to richer solutions. Inclusion ensures those perspectives get heard.
But let's break it down.

- Diversity is recognising and valuing differences – race, gender, age, background, you name it.
- Inclusion is making sure everyone feels respected, valued, and able to contribute.

Together, they're the dynamic duo that helps companies see beyond the obvious. It's like swapping your reading glasses for a kaleidoscope. When you include different perspectives, you get answers you didn't even know you needed.

Leaders: How to Supercharge Curiosity

Curiosity is contagious – especially when leaders lead by example. Here's how to create a curious culture:

1. Lead by Example: Show curiosity in your own work. Ask questions, dig deeper, get excited about new ideas. If you're curious, your team will be too.
2. Create a Safe Environment: Encourage risk-taking without fear of failure. If people feel they can mess up without losing their heads, they'll be more likely to experiment.
3. Provide Resources: Want curiosity to flourish? Give people time, budget, and space to pursue it.
4. Appreciate the Curious: Recognise curiosity even when it doesn't lead to instant results. Sometimes it's about the journey, not the destination.
5. Promote Diversity: The more varied the perspectives, the better the ideas. Mix it up.
6. Open Communication: Make it easy for ideas to flow. Break down silos and create pathways for sharing and collaborating.
7. Tie It to Strategy: Align curiosity with your company's goals. When people see the bigger picture, they'll understand why curiosity matters.

How to Foster a Culture of Curiosity

Want your company to be curious? Here's a quick-start guide:
- Mentorship Programs: Pair curious minds with experienced ones to foster innovation and guidance.
- Innovation Budgets: Set aside money specifically for experimentation – give people the resources to try new things.
- Time for Exploration: Let employees spend time outside their usual roles to explore new ideas.
- Recognition Systems: Reward curiosity. Make sure people know it's not just okay, it's celebrated.
- Interdisciplinary Teams: Break down walls between departments. Innovation loves cross-pollination.
- Flexible Work Environment: Be adaptable, and let your employees explore and innovate without rigid constraints.

The Power of Curiosity in Action

Curiosity isn't just a feel-good bonus – it's the fuel that powers high-performing teams. Here's how it works:
1. Engagement: Curious employees are more engaged because they're constantly exploring and learning.
2. Performance: Curiosity leads to better problem-solving, which means better results.
3. Innovation: A curious team is always coming up with fresh ideas.
4. Adaptability: When the going gets tough, curious employees don't freak out. They embrace the challenge.
5. Growth: Personal and professional growth go hand in hand with curiosity.
6. Workplace Vibe: Curiosity makes the workplace more fun and dynamic – who doesn't love a bit of excitement?
7. Team Connection: When people are curious about each other, they collaborate better.

Curiosity is the secret ingredient that makes everything work better. So, whether you're making carpets or running a Fortune 500, let curiosity be your guide. It's not just about thinking outside the box – it's about shredding the box entirely. Welcome to a world where 'playtime' meets business reality, and everyone – grandkids, Jan, and CEOs – wins.

The Octopus Brain: A Model for Organisational Flexibility

If you've ever felt torn between maintaining tight central control and giving your teams the freedom to innovate, let me introduce you to your new favourite metaphor: the octopus brain. Yep, I'm talking about a creature whose central brain calls the shots but gives each of its eight arms enough autonomy to act independently. Sound familiar? It's basically the dream setup for a modern organisation.

Imagine your company as an octopus. The central brain (aka, the leadership team) sets the overall strategy – like finding food or avoiding predators. But each arm? Oh, those crafty arms have their own mini-brains, letting them act on local information, solve problems in real-time, and adapt to their environment. In the business world, those arms are your teams or departments, each capable of exploring new ideas and solving problems on the fly, while still being connected to the company's broader mission.

This balance – centralised control with decentralised execution – is what every business strives for, but few get right. Just like the octopus, your organisation needs a clear vision (the central brain) while also giving teams the freedom to experiment, innovate, and respond to changing conditions (the arms). It's the sweet spot between micromanaging every decision and letting chaos reign.

Why You Should Care About the Octopus Brain Model

Let's be honest – managing a company's structure is tricky business. Too much centralisation and you stifle creativity. Too little, and things spin out of control. Enter the octopus, which has been thriving with this hybrid system for millions of years. Why? Because it knows how to balance autonomy with alignment.

Here's what we can learn from the octopus brain and how it translates into the business world:
1. Guidance with Freedom: Your leadership sets the direction, but individual teams have the flexibility to figure out how to get there.
2. Local Problem-Solving: Just like an octopus's arm can react to stimuli without checking in with the central brain, your teams can (and should) make decisions without running every little thing up the chain of command.
3. Adaptability at Every Level: The octopus thrives because it's flexible, adapting to its environment on the fly. Your organisation should be able to do the same, pivoting when needed without getting bogged down by red tape.
4. Efficiency with Innovation: This hybrid model means you get the best of both worlds – central efficiency and decentralised creativity. The arms (your teams) can experiment and learn from mistakes, but the central brain keeps everything moving toward the big goals.

How Curiosity Fuels the Octopus Brain Model

Let's add another layer to this metaphor: curiosity. It's the hidden engine that drives this balance between central control and decentralisation. Here's why curiosity is essential:
1. Curiosity Drives Exploration: In the same way that an octopus's arms are constantly probing and exploring, a curious organisation encourages teams to look for new opportunities and solutions. You

want your teams to ask, *"What if we tried this?"*
2. Curiosity Encourages Flexibility: Just as the octopus's arms are flexible in their movements, curiosity makes your team's thinking more flexible. It helps people switch between centralised systems and independent thinking with ease.
3. A Spectrum Approach: Curiosity helps employees see that centralisation vs. decentralisation isn't an either/or choice. It's a spectrum, and different situations call for different approaches.
4. Hybrid Problem-Solving: Curious minds thrive in hybrid models because they enjoy tackling complex problems from multiple angles, just like your company's 'arms' working independently while keeping the big picture in mind.
5. Tech Adoption: Let's be real – new technologies can be scary, but curiosity makes them exciting. Whether it's AI, blockchain, or some other shiny new toy, curious employees will embrace them and figure out how to make them work for your business.

Breaking Down Silos: Curiosity to the Rescue

Every company loves to talk about breaking down silos, but most don't know where to start. Curiosity can help:
1. Fostering Cross-Department Curiosity: When employees are curious, they naturally reach out to other teams, asking, *"Hey, how do you guys do this?"* This cross-departmental curiosity leads to better communication.
2. Sharing Knowledge Freely: Curious employees don't hoard knowledge – they share it. This kind of open exchange naturally dissolves barriers between departments.
3. Collaborative Problem-Solving: Curious minds love collaboration. They know that solving big problems requires input from different departments, and they're willing to roll up their sleeves and work together.
4. Organisational Learning: When curiosity is encouraged, it leads to constant learning, not just for individuals but for the entire compa-

ny. Knowledge doesn't stay stuck in silos; it flows freely, benefiting everyone.
5. Building Bridges: By fostering curiosity about what other teams do, you're encouraging employees to see how their work fits into the larger organisation. They start thinking like an octopus – every arm (team) understands it's part of a bigger body (the company).

A Playbook for Leaders

If you're ready to embrace the octopus brain model and foster curiosity in your organisation, here are some practical steps:
- Lead by Example: Show your curiosity. Ask questions, dig deeper, and be open to new ideas. Your teams will follow your lead.
- Create Psychological Safety: Make sure your people feel safe to explore, experiment, and fail. No one's going to be curious if they're terrified of messing up.
- Provide Resources: Give your teams the time, budget, and support they need to explore new ideas.
- Reward Curiosity: Celebrate those who are pushing the boundaries, even if they don't always hit a home run. It's the effort that counts.
- Encourage Cross-Department Interaction: Create opportunities for different teams to work together and share ideas. The more they interact, the more they'll learn from each other.

Curiosity: The Antidote to Conservatism.

Not Just in Business, but in Politics Too

I've just had one of those lightbulb moments, the kind that slaps you in the face when you least expect it. Here I am, knee-deep in *The Net Curiosity Score*—yes, the book that's taken chunks of my soul and even more cups of coffee—and it hits me. This isn't just a toolkit for sparking curiosity and innovation in business. No, it's something bigger. It's a sly, stealthy antidote to conservatism, and I don't mean only in the boardroom.

Think about it.

Conservatism—whether it's buttoned up in a corporate suit or dressed in political rhetoric—shares a certain DNA. It's all about keeping things just as they are, grasping tightly to the 'good old days,' and trying to manage a world that's spinning faster than they'd like. It's cozy, yes, but also paralyzed by fear of what's next. Businesses that cling to ancient models? They fall behind. We've all seen it. But what about politics? What happens when governments—or worse, entire societies—refuse to evolve, to stay curious about the changing world around them?

It's the same tragic formula: stagnation, slow decay into irrelevance, and a creeping fear of the future.

That's where *The Net Curiosity Score* sneaks in like a well-timed antidote. The book is a manifesto for change, a call to arms for curiosity, and an exploration of pushing boundaries in business. But it's more than that. What I've realized is that it's also a roadmap out of political conservatism—a guide for any organization, any government, even any society, on how to beat back the looming shadow of stagnation.

Conservatism's Real Fear: Curiosity

Conservatives—whether in the boardroom or in office—don't like to move forward. They want to stay put, always longing for 'better days' in some mythical past. They fear change, they fear innovation, and most of all, they fear curiosity. Because here's the thing: curiosity breeds questions, and questions shake up the status quo. They disrupt the comfort of the past and open up the terrifying possibility that maybe—just maybe—the future doesn't belong to them.

Curiosity is dangerous to conservatism because it's unpredictable. It pulls the rug out from under the idea that things should stay as they are, that old ways are always best, and that the future can be neatly boxed up in the familiar and comfortable. 'Curiosity is, in great and generous minds, the first passion and the last', wrote Samuel Johnson, and there's truth in that. Conservative thinking struggles with curiosity because it's an act of rebellion against the past, against control. And nothing scares conservatives more than loss of control.

But the Future Doesn't Care About Your Control

The uncomfortable truth is that the future is coming whether we like it or not. And the only way to navigate it—let alone thrive in it—is through curiosity. By daring to ask tough questions, to experiment, and to unlearn what we thought we knew. I've said it a thousand times in business: *The Net Curiosity Score* isn't just about survival, but about fostering a mindset that will thrive in what's to come.

Let's look at politics. Conservatism thrives on a fear of the unknown. The future, according to the conservative narrative, is a Pandora's box filled with threats: immigration, technology, social change. And the answer? Stand still. Look backward. Re-create some golden age that's mostly fiction, a fabricated past where everything was simpler and more manageable. Sound familiar? It's the same tactic used by businesses clinging to old models while the world shifts under their feet.

The problem with this approach is that the world *never* stands still. Technology advances, cultural norms shift, and global dynamics evolve. You can long for the past all you want, but the future doesn't care. It keeps coming, faster and faster. And the only people who can face it head-on are those who stay curious—the ones who look ahead, ask questions, and have the courage to adapt.

Curiosity as the Antidote

So, here's my realization: *The Net Curiosity Score* isn't just a playbook for companies trying to stay relevant. It's a call to action for anyone—whether you're a CEO, a politician, or a curious citizen—to reject fear, to engage with the world around you, and to welcome the messy, unpredictable, and thrilling ride into the future. Curiosity is the antidote to stagnation. It's the cure for control, fear, and standing still.

Take, for example, the words of Albert Einstein, who famously said, 'The important thing is not to stop questioning. Curiosity has its own reason for existing.' Curiosity is the lifeblood of progress; it's what lets us dream, innovate, and evolve. And yet, conservatives in both business and politics shy away from it, viewing it as a threat rather than an opportunity.

Here's the thing: to stand still is to wither. Societies that cling to the past, fearing progress, will fall behind. But those that embrace curiosity, that ask, 'What if?' and 'What's next?'—they'll be the ones that thrive. History shows us that the biggest breakthroughs happen when we dare to challenge the status quo, to step beyond the comfort of tradition and explore the unknown.

Curiosity Is Liberation

Curiosity isn't just about innovation. It's about liberation. It frees us from the constraints of outdated thinking, from the shackles of fear. It empowers us to question, to explore, to imagine new possibilities. In a world where conservatism seeks to control and contain, curiosity is the radical force that says, 'No, we can be better. We can move forward.'
When I started writing *The Net Curiosity Score*, I thought it was a guide for helping companies survive. But now I see it's more than that. It's a manifesto for anyone who refuses to stand still, who won't be held back by the past. It's for those who dare to ask questions, challenge the status quo, and leap into the uncertain, unpredictable future with a grin on their face.

The future belongs to the curious. And maybe, just maybe, that's what conservatives fear the most.

Final Thoughts

Like the octopus, your organisation can balance central control with the freedom to explore. It's not an easy balance to strike, but with the right mix of curiosity and autonomy, your company can be as adaptable – and as successful – as the octopus in its environment. Keep that central brain sharp, but don't forget to let the arms stretch and explore. You never know what innovations might be lurking just beyond reach.

The AI Spectre: Scrambled Eggs for Thought

In a softly lit room, surrounded by old friends, we sat together as we often do, reminiscing, laughing about life's small joys. It's what we do – talk about the kids, the grandkids, the chaotic beauty of it all. Our minds, though marked by time, are still sharp, still curious, still reaching for something just beyond the horizon.

But this time, the conversation took a twist. The topic of Artificial Intelligence crept in, and just like that, all eyes were on me. *Rik, the expert in all things future*, they seemed to say, leaning in as the rain drummed on the window outside. It was time for the hot seat.

"Can AI really be creative?" one friend asked, eyebrows raised, challenging me with the ease of a well-worn debate.

I took a sip of my wine, thinking. AI creative? It was a question I'd answered a hundred times, but here, amidst the quiet hum of shared history, it felt different. "Maybe," I started, "AI is like a musician who can't stop playing cover songs. It doesn't create in the same way we do. But," I paused, "it's more than just an imitator. It's a remix artist. A thief and a muse all at once."

The room filled with scepticism. Chomsky's ghost sat at the table. "Plagiarism," someone declared with a dramatic flair, "AI's nothing but a digital thief, stealing from human creativity."

I laughed under my breath, the rain still tapping like a soft metronome. "Maybe," I said, glancing out the window, "but aren't we all remix artists? Aren't all our so-called original ideas just echoes of something that came before?"

The room quieted. They didn't buy it. I didn't mind.

AI and Curiosity: The Real Deal

I'm not here to say AI is going to be the next Picasso. But here's what I do know – AI isn't killing curiosity. It's feeding it. Yeah, you heard me right. Augmented Curiosity is the future, and AI is the tool that's going to supercharge it.

Here's how:
- Explorative Curiosity: You want to explore new ideas, new concepts, new fields? AI is your new best friend. It sifts through data faster than any human, spotting patterns we'd miss. It's like having an all-access pass to the world's biggest library and getting to skip the lines.
- Empathic Curiosity: AI can analyse social dynamics, dig deep into human behaviour, and help us understand others in ways we never could before. It doesn't feel empathy, but it sure can teach us a thing or two about what makes people tick.
- Goal-Oriented Curiosity: You've got a problem to solve? AI can simulate scenarios, test theories, and predict outcomes with precision. It's like having a brainstorming partner who never sleeps.

So, no. AI isn't here to steal your job or dull your creativity. It's here to give you the tools to go further, faster, and with more depth. The human-AI combo is what's going to tackle the big stuff – the wicked problems that keep us up at night. Climate change? Healthcare innovation? These aren't things you solve by yourself. These are team efforts, and guess what? AI is on the team.

Generative AI: The Remix Artist of the Future

If AI had a theme song, it'd be *Remix to Ignition*. Here's why. Generative AI isn't a creator in the traditional sense – it doesn't wake up one day with a brilliant new idea. What it does is even more interesting. It takes all the input we've fed it – millions of data points, patterns, structures – and spins something new out of them. Just like we do.

- Pattern Recognition: Just like we spot trends, AI does too, but on steroids.
- Knowledge Generation: It creates new insights, new content, but all based on what already exists. It's the ultimate collaborator, taking what we've built and running with it.
- Creativity: Is it creative? Depends on how you define creativity. If creativity is just a rehash of old ideas in new ways, then sure, AI is creative. If it's about dreaming up something truly, radically new, then that's still on us.

But hey, aren't we just magpies too? We take bits and pieces from everything around us and call it something new. AI's just better at sorting through the pieces.

The Logic of Lions and the Wonder of Why

On a crisp autumn morning, my 3-year-old granddaughter nestled beside me, her tiny body warm against mine as we sifted through a stack of books bursting with bright colors and wild adventures. Today's journey would be a tour of the animal kingdom, a world of the big, small, fierce, and gentle. Her curious fingers pointed to the first creature on the page—a long-snouted figure.

'That's an anteater,' I said, watching as she examined it with a seriousness that only a child can have. Those big, wondering eyes drank it in, her mind absorbing every detail in the way kids do, mapping new creatures to her little world.

I reached to turn the page, but her small hand stopped me. She stared at the anteater a moment longer, processing whatever mystery it held, and then nodded, satisfied with her introduction. We turned to the next page, and there we were—right in the heart of Africa, with lions standing tall against the golden savannah, and hyenas slinking in the shadows. Her finger shot toward each animal, studying them in turn.

'What about that one? Can a lion eat it?' she asked, her voice full of innocent awe.

'Yes,' I replied.

'And that one?' Her finger hovered over a gazelle, then a zebra.

'Yes, they could.'

The questions kept coming, each time punctuated with my answer. Her curiosity was on fire, each piece of information falling into place as she built her understanding of the animal world. Then the questions slowed, and a quiet settled in. She was thinking, processing it all with that boundless kid-brain of hers. And after what felt like a century of silence, she turned to me, her big eyes full of a question that would knock the sense right out of me.

'Why do we call it a lion when it's an animal-eater?'

I blinked, my mind reeling from the pure, razor-sharp logic of her question. Why do we call it a lion? She had stripped away language, ignoring names and meanings we took for granted, and reduced it to essence.

My brain scrambled for an answer, something to explain this new truth she'd unearthed.

And there, in that quiet morning glow, I found myself wandering into thoughts about AI. Could a machine, no matter how advanced, ever reach this level of creative questioning? Could AI someday surprise us, not with flawless algorithms or vast knowledge, but with the sort of wild, illogical leap that only a child's mind could take? Her question left me smiling, awestruck by the simplicity and beauty of curiosity—and realizing just how little we know about the nature of thinking itself.

I looked down at her, my own question still unanswered. Her wide eyes sparkled with quiet satisfaction, as if she had already found a truth beyond words—a truth she knew I might never fully grasp.

'Well,' I finally said, 'maybe someday we'll meet a lion and ask him ourselves.'

And with that, we moved on, but the question lingered. Maybe, I thought, the magic lies in just asking.

Finally: The Last Raindrop

Weeks passed since that night with friends, but the conversation stuck with me like the last raindrop clinging to my windshield. I'm driving home, the rain painting abstract patterns on the glass, and I've got a podcast playing. *A Life in Lyrics,* Paul Muldoon and Sir Paul McCartney, the legend himself, talking about how he wrote *Yesterday.*

Not my favourite McCartney song, but iconic, right? Muldoon asks him, "How did you come up with that melody?" And McCartney, in that familiar Liverpool accent, says, "I dreamt it."

He dreamt it. Woke up, stumbled to the piano, and there it was – one of the most famous melodies ever written, like it had floated down from the stars into his head. A gift from the universe, he says.

And suddenly, it hit me. Creativity isn't this sacred, untouchable thing. It's scrambled eggs. It's a remix of echoes, of melodies we've heard somewhere before, pulled together into something new. McCartney even thought he'd stolen it at first. He asked Lennon, he asked George Martin. "Familiar," they said. "But no, this is yours. You've just pieced together the chords you've been hearing your whole life."

Isn't that what AI does? It pieces together the chords of the universe, the bits and bytes of data we've fed it, and it gives us something new. Not perfect, not original in the way we think of it, but new nonetheless. As the rain kept falling, the wipers slicing through the droplets, I couldn't help but smile. Creativity, AI, life – it's all just scrambled eggs.

A Word of Thanks

A business book without a word of thanks? I wouldn't dare. Not because I'm one to follow the well-worn paths. By now, any attentive reader will have realised that this is not exactly my style. I love breaking through established formulas. I cherish the unexpected – for both writer and reader. Somewhere in this book, didn't I mention... how I try to pull you, the reader, out of your comfort zone? How I aim to make each little piece here a pebble in the stream of your consciousness, creating ripples that may or may not collide and blend? Still, I write a very traditional word of thanks. I am, after all, a friendly and well-mannered boy. Gratitude is part of that.

Outside, the weather is much like my writing: unpredictable and ever-changing. After two books, I've built a wonderful relationship with LannooCampus, and I've had the fortune of being surrounded by amazing people like Niels, Marije, Susan, and Steve, who have patiently endured my whims, shaped my wild ideas, and gently nudged me when I felt stuck or when I thought I should start another book. I'm deeply grateful to them for that.

So, a word of thanks. Who else should I thank?

The team at Microsoft Netherlands back in 2015, for without them, I might never have started writing books – let alone this one. Thank you, Pieter, Marcel, Nancy, Martin, Sandra, and so many others for this.

Then there was Ivy, who invited me to speak at an event called the "SAS Curiosity Forum 2019," where I gave my very first keynote on curiosity. Eternal thanks to Ivy and her then-CEO Jeroen.

Thanks to so many Programme Directors at London Business School, who accepted – and even encouraged – my stubborn unpredictability, bringing me into contact with so many top companies and industries, where I've learned so much.

A special thank you to Peter, who sat in the audience when I first casually mentioned the Net Curiosity Score as a KPI at the end of a short speech. I left the audience with a bit of homework, asking them to think about that KPI. Peter whispered to me afterwards, "This is a great topic for a book." His words were both incredibly motivating and, at the same time, a little paralysing.

Thanks to the hundreds of participants in workshops who have challenged and inspired me time and time again.

Thank you to my dear friends Adelitha, Maartje, Crijn, Viviane, Suzanne, Claire, Beau, Bas... from Het Sprekershuys, who take such good care of me. You make the most wonderful job in the world a little less lonely and allow me to fully devote myself to writing and creating keynotes.

Thanks to my parents. I was a dreamy child. They allowed that. Thanks to them, I can proudly say I've read an entire encyclopedia from A to Z – literally. Every two weeks, a new volume would arrive from the encyclopedia they bought for their children, and I devoured each one, curious from the first page to the last. My insatiable hunger for knowledge, in every field, was born there.

Thank you, Jan, for teaching me that it's not just curiosity, but a deep craving for the new – nieuwsgierigheid. (not to be translated, sorry folks)

Lastly, I thank my children, Lore and Lisse, and my grandchildren for their pure, uninhibited curiosity, which inspires me more than words can say.

Rik